Praise for FUEL YOUR BUSINESS

"Reading **Fuel Your Business** is like sitting down for a lively conversation with one of the most energetic people you'll ever meet. Gina Soleil, in her centered and thoughtful way, takes you on the journey to understanding that your business is not just a separate entity you need to work on, but rather a living, breathing creature that needs to be nurtured just like the human beings it is made of. When business leaders escape their preconceptions and embrace her energy-centered approach, we'll all enjoy a transformation in American business culture."

—James Matheson, president and partner, Network Medics, Inc.

"Above the often neglected or simply unseen landscape between personal and organizational transformation, Soleil shines her light on the deeper truths—and shadows—of management, and, indeed, true leadership. This book captures in living color what often passes for black-and-white stills that leave people cold. Soleil makes business ethics sing with soul. She champions the radical yet rooted-in-the-human-core possibility of our vast business tools and modern machinery serving us—not the other way around."

—Rick Bernardo, assistant professor, Business Management Ethics/Organizational Leadership/Cyber-tech Ethics, St. Mary's University of MN

"Business is powered by energy. By shifting, nurturing, and accelerating it, you create a renewable energy source more valuable than all the oil wells on the planet, every uncut diamond, and every ounce of platinum in the galaxy. Get ready for the rocketship ride of your life as **Fuel Your Business** launches you and your company into a whole new universe of possibility and profitability."

—Jeanine Thompson, business energy expert, president of Jeanine Thompson, LLC

"Gina Soleil moves through life with a beautiful understanding of human energy. She brings awareness to the knowledge that how we move through our daily lives energetically will affect us physically. Through her book **Fuel Your Business** she bridges the divide of understanding from personal into business. She guides us through the appreciation that business culture is personal, and to move forward with success we need to close that gap."

—Emily Hall, body intuitive, founder of Your Intuitive Body

"It's rare that in your life you get to meet a person with the intensity of purpose as strong as the noonday sun, and the drive to accomplish that purpose so strong that a team of wild horses could not stop them; Gina Soleil is one of those people. As a colleague and friend, I have found that Soleil is unwavering in her desire to make things better than she found them—in both her business and her personal life. She not only teaches the principles in her book **Fuel Your Business**, she lives them! Look out, Corporate America, times have changed, and Gina Soleil just wrote the new rulebook on how to run a business."

—Jason Thomas, senior Web developer, RBA Consulting

"**Fuel Your Business** is a long-awaited wedding of the business world and the field of human energy. In this accessible and engaging book, she shares a practical map for how to use the principles of energy work in order to improve not only the bottom line, but also humanity."

—Juliana Keen, founder of Next Step Consulting

fuel your business

fuel your business

How to Energize People, Ignite Action, and Drive Profits

gina soleil

CAREER
PRESS

Pompton Plains, N.J.

Fuel Your Business

Edited by Jodi Brandon
Typeset by Eileen Munson
Cover design by Ty Nowicki
Printed in the U.S.A.

To order this title, please call toll-free 1-800-CAREER-1 (NJ and Canada: 201-848-0310) to order using VISA or MasterCard, or for further information on books from Career Press.

The Career Press, Inc.
220 West Parkway, Unit 12
Pompton Plains, NJ 07444
www.careerpress.com

Library of Congress Cataloging-in-Publication Data
Soleil, Gina.
    Fuel your business : how to energize people, ignite action, and drive profits / by Gina Soleil.
        pages cm
    Includes bibliographical references and index.
    ISBN 978-1-60163-296-8 -- ISBN 978-1-60163-495-5 (ebook)
        1. Organizational behavior. 2. Corporate culture. 3. Employee motivation.
    4. Management. I. Title.

HD58.7.S6745 2014
658.3'14--dc23

2013039023

To my daughter, Gabby, who shines truth and light, and is the essence of the pure joy of life. I love you more than the world is round.

acknowledgments

My life has been filled with people who have fueled my soul and taught me that life is not about the destination, but the journey of experiences that lead us to the finish line. These people have reminded me to just sit back and enjoy the ride—because it's the moments we experience along the way where real joy lives and life happens.

The first of those people are my mom and dad: two people who (thankfully) gave me an unconventional upbringing. Because of you, I grew up always knowing I could be anything, do anything, and become anything my soul desired. My dad was the one who reminded me that I am a bird worthy and deserving to be free and fly. He taught me that in life the beauty of the rose is not in the color of the petal but in the prick of the thorn. He taught me that if I follow my passion, my truth, and my love, everything I need in life always follows. My mom taught me that in life everything happens for a reason. She has always been there when my heart hurt most. And through her intuitive gifts, I learned mine. She is the woman I laugh with until I cry, and whom I seek out when I need to go home.

The two other people in my family who have been instrumental in my journey are my Grandma and my daughter. My Grandma, who passed away last summer at the beautiful age of 96, taught me that life is worth living, and that there is always enough in life to love and be inspired by. She taught me to enjoy every experience life has to offer, and keep moving forward. My daughter, Gabby, continues to show me unexplainable love, light, and truth—it's through her laugh, her hugs, and her inspirational acts of joy that I'm reminded of the purity of life.

I have a number of amazing friends who have stood by my side while I began the journey that opened the doors to this book:

Jennifer Hovelsrud, who reviewed every word of the manuscript, encouraged me every step of the way, and always believed that this message was going out to the world by the millions. Her intellect, love, friendship, and willingness to take on this project as a reviewer— during a time of life when adding just one more thing seemed virtually impossible—helped make this book what it is today.

Maureen Klehr, who reminded me to write this book for the people of the world who are ready for the knowledge, and that every word written will speak to every person to whom the words are intended—perfectly.

Jason Thomas, a.k.a. JACK, who has been my friend and unwavering supporter through the most audacious times of my life thus far. Always there willing to do whatever it takes to make shit happen, and never doubting anything I believed in, no matter how outrageous the rest of the world thought I was.

And Shelly Harvey, who helped jumpstart my journey of joy, and who embraced her own joy journey with courage. She was the first person from the corporate world to read the first words of this book. Her response, "Oh my gosh, it's so good. I just want more," was a confidence boost that accelerated fearless writing.

My education and business experience has also been filled with people to whom I will forever be grateful:

Louise Miner, my graduate school professor and advisor, a woman who helped me begin to realize the talent that was inside me just waiting to be let loose and given to the world.

And my grad school girlfriends, who, during our time together, gave me the support that allowed me to spread my wings and fly.

James Matheson, Kevin Calgren, and Patrick Massey, the owners of Network Medics, my friends. These guys were the first clients who embraced my authentic self without question. You are role models for all businesses, and you are changing this world.

And Career Press, a publisher with a soul, and the business that took a risk on me because they knew that the world was ready to experience the intersection between business and energy.

Lastly, Emily Hall, my best friend, and the greatest healer of our time. It was Emily who pushed me to write this book—for that I will always be grateful. Together we are bringing our gifts to the world, and helping to move humanity forward toward peace every step of the way.

There are countless numbers of people who have impacted my life in amazing ways. Family, friends, and colleagues—all people who have touched my soul in beautiful ways. I acknowledge all of you and thank all of you from every part of my heart. I could literally fill a book of gratitude for all the people who have touched my life.

I love you all.

contents

The Eight Principles of Business

Everything is energy and that's all there is to it. Match the frequency of the reality you want, and you cannot help but get that reality. It can be no other way. This is not philosophy. This is physics.

—Albert Einstein

Understanding the truth of human energy, and the power it has in this world, changed my life. It has allowed me to move forward in this world fearlessly and with heart, and it also made my business stronger. The knowledge of human energy is transformative, and it opens doors of exploration, discovery, and profound experiences that will catapult you and your business into a new reality—a reality that fuels people with the energy they so desperately need, ignites action, and drives business profits to new levels.

This book is the result of my research findings on human energy, and my experience in business and in life throughout the years. It's for leaders who understand that people are the engine of their business, and who are ready to embrace new principles and truths about what drives energy, action, and profits. I'm going to take you on a journey, give you an inside tour of your business and the minds of the people who work in it, and show you exactly how to create a culture that fuels the greatest resource of our time: human energy. This book is your guide to creating a high-performing business that gets results, by creating a business culture that's fueled with healthy human energy. It's your pathway to greater levels of growth and innovation. This book is the new engagement and performance strategy for business in today's world.

Introduction: The Journey Begins

The Introduction introduces you to the human energy crisis, and explains why people are so exhausted and energy-depleted in today's world. It reveals the business chakra system, and introduces you to the Eight Principles of Business—a framework that sets the stage for the entire book.

Chapter 1—Principle #1: Functional Leaders Drive Profits

Chapter 1 exposes the truth about dysfunctional leadership in business. You'll have an opportunity to take the Toxic Leadership Quiz to see if your business is suffering from unhealthy energy, and you'll get a step-by-step leadership development plan that is guaranteed to start fueling leaders with healthy energy that gets results.

Chapter 2—Principle #2: Vision and Purpose Ignite Forward Momentum

Chapter 2 is all about getting your business to its ultimate destination: a healthy bottom line. You'll learn how to create a destination map, and leverage your map to inspire people in a way that ignites profitable action from part-time Joe all the way through to the CEO.

Chapter 3—Principle #3: Truth and Clarity Motivate Action

Chapter 3 reveals how truth and clarity ignite the must-have action businesses need to achieve sustainable profitability. You'll learn the communication techniques that inspire and motivate, and what traditional techniques to stay away from—techniques that demotivate people and derail the most well-thought-out business strategies.

Chapter 4—Principle #4: People Are Driven to Live Out a Purpose

Chapter 4 is about individual purpose and how creating opportunities for people to be part of something greater than themselves ignites the drive that every business needs to move forward. You'll learn how to harness individual purpose to take your business to the next level.

Chapter 5—Principle #5: Freedom Turns Ideas and Vision Into Reality

Ideas and vision are attained through attitude—also called an internal brand. Chapter 5 addresses the internal brand of your business, and shows you how ideas and vision are attained through an *anything is possible* attitude; you'll learn how to get everyone in your business living an *anything is possible* attitude within every area of your business.

Chapter 6—Principle #6: Creative Expression Fuels Change and Growth

Change and growth are propelled forward by environment, and it's the environment that fuels people to move the business forward. Chapter 6 addresses personal power, boundaries, and how understanding the term *energy vampire* will automatically transform your business environment into a haven of productivity.

Chapter 7—Principle #7: Human Connectivity Is the Source of Energy

We are all one, interconnected through energy. Chapter 7 addresses how owning our own story, putting people first, and running a business on the philosophy of **DO NO EVIL** will turn energetically toxic business environments into energetically healthy ones.

Chapter 8—Principle #8: Humanity Is the Future

Improving the health and well-being of humanity is the only answer to preserving a world that will continue to fuel business. Chapter 8 addresses the concepts of collective responsibility, collective strength, and both internal and external social responsibility. You'll get the plan for how to fuel the energy of your business by taking care of the basic needs of humanity.

Conclusion: A Letter to the World

The book concludes with a letter to the world, a letter that encourages and inspires every reader to take each of the **Eight Principles of Business** forward into their business.

Appendix: The Energy Assessment

At the back of the book there is an energy assessment that allows you to measure your own businesses energy level. Is it toxic? Is it healthy? What work can you do right now to start getting the results you want? Take the assessment and find out your next steps.

Let's Get Started

By reading this book, you'll learn how to harness energy for yourself and the people who make up your business. You'll learn how to build a strong business culture that energizes people, ignites action, and drives profits by applying process and systems thinking, as well as energy-producing best practices, to everyday operations.

For every action there is a reaction in our world. My hope is that you'll use this knowledge to create the change inside your business that will impact humanity for years to come. With that, my friends, let's get started.

introduction

The Journey Begins

With a coffee, a smartphone (sometimes two), keys, and a bag of some sort in hand, Michael enters my office with a look of exhaustion and sinks into a chair with a sigh. He begins sharing his typical day. Walking into his office each morning he thinks, *Here I go again—eight meetings, seven critical e-mails, 30 other e-mails awaiting my response, and a personal life that's falling apart.* Barely able to make it from one meeting to the next, he's exhausted, and his lack of energy is impacting his focus, drive, and confidence. The 14-hour days are becoming unbearable, and his tolerance for dealing with minutiae is decreasing each time he walks through the doors of his office. His performance is on the downslide.

The image of Michael represents most people working in your business. Exhaustion is a trend that's growing so fast that we now have a name for it: the **human energy crisis**. From the United Nations to the Ivy League, human energy is becoming the hot topic of discussion and research. This crisis is impacting our relationships, our physical bodies, and the perception we have of the world. This energy crisis has now crept into business like termites seeking out their next home. People no longer have the energy they once had to be fully engaged, productive, and innovative. Bottom line? People are exhausted.

So what's causing the energy crisis? Let's face it: Life is tough, and our technologically connected, plugged-in world doesn't make it any easier to stay on top of our game. In fact, this connected world of instant gratification that fuels our addiction for information is often the very reason we can't seem to pull ourselves out of bed in the morning. I call this the morning *ugh* syndrome. The increase in demand for our attention often becomes overwhelming. We desperately try to catch our breath as the five e-mails that just came through crush any hope of having free time for the next month. Then there's the pressure of society. We're running kids from one activity to the next, getting multiple degrees, and buying bigger, buying more, and buying better things to show the world we have arrived. Then there's what you call "relationships." Wait, those still exist? We've become experts at going through the motions, staying in relationships that are "safe" and "status quo," because we're too exhausted to do anything about them. And if we're not in a relationship, we're on a constant online search for "big love." Oh, did I mention that all of this happens in just one day? So, in complete exhaustion, we give ourselves a pep talk and keep on keepin' on.

When we get into the office each day, it's game time. As we are battling exhaustion, we must ensure that we fit in, play by the rules, follow unsaid, unwritten cultural norms, engage in politics, "package" our words appropriately, and don't ever screw up! I haven't even touched on the challenges of egos, diversity, working with people we don't like, or leadership dysfunction. We spend our days thinking, "I want more in life," but we stay put because of the golden handcuffs, security, and the fact that we're too tired to make a change. It's no wonder that after a day's worth of work we're exhausted.

Then people arrive to work, and the business asks them be more engaged: "Give us more of your discretionary energy; be more involved, productive, creative, and strategic." In frustration the business asks people, "Why won't you participate? Why don't you listen? Why won't you perform? Damn it, we have strategic plans that need to be executed." The answer: your people are tired, exhausted, beat up, and they don't have any more energy to give.

Welcome to business in today's world. The energy crisis breeds self-doubt, hinders focus, prevents people from accomplishing their best, stifles creativity, dissipates tolerance, and drives healthcare costs through the roof. In the United States alone, workplace stress is a $300 billion cost to the healthcare industry (American Institute of Stress), obesity is another $192 billion (Trust for America's Health), and chronic disease, including heart disease, diabetes, and stroke, is a $616 billion cost to healthcare (WebMD). People are tired, sick, and dying. That's not harsh; that's reality. (I should warn you: I will never package things in pretty bows, and I will always call a spade a spade.) This reality is the baggage every one of us carries to work each day. If you're running a business, small or large, this reality is your greatest threat. If this doesn't describe your business, congratulations! Now I would ask you to question whether that's truth or denial. The brutal reality is that this is the truth for 99 percent of businesses today. The energy crisis is resulting in mediocre strategy, decreased engagement, and less-than-stellar profits. Businesses are wasting thousands, if not millions, of dollars on engagement and management strategies in an effort to revive and refuel performance, only to find that they keep getting more of the same: a big fat bill for strategies that aren't working.

Before we go too far into doom and gloom, let me tell you there is a solution. If you can refuel your people with the energy they so desperately need, you'll revive your business tenfold. It's not difficult—it's just energy. According to Einstein, "Everything is energy and that's all there is to it. Match the frequency of the reality you want and you cannot help but get that reality. It can be no other way. This is not philosophy. This is physics." I have to say, I am in love with Einstein—partly because of his hair, but mostly because of his audacious brilliance that he fearlessly brought to our world in order to prove us all wrong.

Let me be clear on the topic of energy: I'm not talking about eating better, sleeping more, working out, or adding another "must do" to your schedule. Yes, all those things are important to being a healthy human being, but when I'm addressing human energy, I'm addressing the energetic frequencies that radiate from your body and impact those around you and the rest of the world. Modern science has proven that we are all made of energy. No longer can we argue the fact that we all have energy that radiates from our bodies like exhaust fumes from a truck, or like the steam from a freshly baked apple pie; you can't see or smell it, but it's everywhere, evoking emotions and thoughts of either disgust or delight. We can compare your personal energy to garlic, an herb that has the ability to seep through the pores of our skin, filling a room with its aroma. People either love you or hate you for it; they run toward you or can't get away from you fast enough.

Here's an example of how unhealthy energy looks in your everyday life. Think about that person you know who, for some reason, makes you want to run for the hills as soon as she comes toward you. This is a person, when you're around her, who makes you feel as though you just got slimed. Her presence makes you feel suffocated, depleted, and exhausted. It's as though this person has the ability to take any negative emotion she might be thinking or feeling in the moment and dump it over your head until you have to jump around and shake it off. Ugh! Some of you might be thinking about your mother (just kidding, Mom), or that colleague you dread having on team projects. But I have bad news: The brutal reality is that for some people, this person is you! Fact. And if you're exhausted, and being ruled by sabotaging thoughts and emotions, the energy you're giving to other people is toxic and is wreaking havoc on everything within your world.

Science has proven that energy is inside us and all around us. Amazing technological advances have even given us the ability to physically measure human energy: ECG (electrocardiogram) measures electrical energy currents from the heart; EEG (electroencephalogram) measures energy currents from the brain; lie detectors measure energy from the skin; the SQUID (superconducting quantum interference device) measures energy fields around the body, not even touching the person being measured. (*Hands of Light* by Barbara Brennan) Science has even gone a step further and theorized the "butterfly effect": the idea that the energy frequency from one thought, word, or action has the ability to create a natural disaster on the other side of the world. How many of us wake up each morning and say, "I have to be aware of what I think today because I don't want to cause a tsunami in Indonesia"? But according to science, that is a reality. More obvious is the fact that our thoughts can cause a tsunami in our own lives.

Through energy, everything in our world is connected and one. For those of you who like analogies, this can be compared to a body of water: Your business is like a flowing river, and every person inside your business is a water molecule that makes the river whole. Every thought, word, action, and emotion from each person changes the molecular structure of the river. Now, if you have a bunch of Yodas working for you, this can be absolutely fantastic! If you don't have Yoda on the payroll, and you're like most businesses that have normal human beings who are exhausted working for you, your river is polluted with the same green slime from the previous example—and you can't eat the fish! If you want to drive profits and improve business efficiencies and morale, you have to figure out how to get every person inside your business operating on healthy human energy. It doesn't matter how tight your process, systems, and management structure might be, if you have toxic human energy being dumped into the river, and people don't have the energy to perform, you won't achieve squat!

I know you didn't buy this book to get a science lesson on the theory of relativity and the butterfly effect. You want to know how to fuel your business, how to energize people, ignite action, and drive profits. You want your business to perform at higher levels—make more, do more, be more. Let's quickly align on the word *business*.

Business is a word that is applied to politics, religion, and private or public commerce. I use the word *business* to describe any entity trying to drive profits into an organization. Profits are dollars or participation from people outside the business that generate what a business needs to move forward. If you're reading this book, you want more profits. If you want more profits, your biggest ally is the science of energy. The truth of the matter is, business is science. In fact, your business is a giant Petri dish for proving the accuracy of physics—energy. Your business is all about cause and effect. You perform experiments every day by changing processes, introducing initiatives, bringing different people into the equation, moving people around, and inventing new products—all scientific experiments intended to prove out your hypothesis of how to make more money!

You most likely already get the fact that we are all made of energy, that we are all energetically interconnected, and that human energy has the ability to make or break profit. In fact, as an intelligent human being, you may also follow many advances in modern-day science and say, "Makes sense." I call this the "get it" factor. But here's the crazy thing: The minute we step into a business it's as though we step into a time machine and begin thinking like we're Isaac Newton—everything is solid, individual, and systematic.

Quite frankly, it's amazing that we get anything done or make any profits at all. It's as though someone is standing at the doors of every business waiting to zap us with a neuralyzer while saying, "You will not remember anything that makes sense for how to run a business in the current world. Welcome back to 1885." (Thank you, *Men in Black*, for help with that analogy!) For some reason, while inside the business, we completely forget about human energy and modern-day science. We start thinking that people are solid cogs inside a giant machine. We have strategy meetings to talk about human capital processes, systematic approaches to engagement, and linear initiatives to build morale and communication platforms. Wow, that's a mouthful! We pride ourselves on building PowerPoint presentations, having top-secret management sessions, and implementing complex talent development systems to get people to behave the way *we* believe will drive results. Even approaches to culture are systematic: *Let's get a bunch of leaders together in a room and teach them how to say this, do that, say this, do that.* Then we ask ourselves, why are we consistently spending thousands, if not millions, of dollars on trying to improve our business and drive profits? Sweetheart, this ain't rocket science. All you have to do is turn around and see that you have human beings running your business—not cogs.

Let me be clear: Process is important and critically necessary. I'm not proposing that we do away with the structure needed to keep a business moving forward. I am stating that businesses today are suffering from a severe case of analysis paralysis (a.k.a. overkill), and neglecting their most valuable resource: human energy. Just ask yourself, when was the last time you spent countless hours working on a presentation or project to see it go absolutely nowhere? Part of the problem is that exhaustion is inhibiting us from making thoughtful decisions. We're all on autopilot. "Let's do it this way because this is how we always do it, and we're too tired to change, too exhausted to fight the culture." A business will inevitably spend less, become more efficient, and make more money if it starts re-fueling the energy of its people from the inside out. Process for process's sake does not drive financial accumulation, people do. If people have no energy to make process happen, all you have is a bunch of words and symbols on paper that result in frustration, disappointment, and a lack of trust. Sound familiar?

Now let's go back to science. Remember the fundamental principle: We are all interconnected, and the energy created by our thoughts and emotions has significant power over our business and our lives. So, to fuel your business, you have to address the thoughts and emotions driving your business. Your business runs on people, and the emotions and thoughts of the people who work for your business drive every action, process, and profit opportunity your business has. If this seems too "touchy-feely," think about a time when you did something, anything at all, that had absolutely no thought or emotion involved; a time when you had no thoughts or emotions running through you. If you're human, it's not possible. Even the state of simply "being" is a state of emotional recognition that you are present with what's going on around you in the moment. Thoughts and emotions drive all aspects of our reality. Every word and every action that is used to run your business is driven by human thought, emotion, and energy. Again, this is great if you have Yodas running your business, but remember the Michael story from the first paragraph. It's Michael whom you have on your payroll. Here's another fact: You can't create healthy thoughts and emotions inside your business by turning leaders into cogs. Ditch the workshops. You have to address the energy deficiency within each individual leader running your business, create a business operating system that is designed to circulate healthy energy throughout the business, and build an accountability practice that acts as a consistent air purifier, refueling the energy of employees—an energy ecosystem you'll learn how to build throughout this book.

The Eight Principles of Business

Here's the jump. Grab your parachute, because I'm about to take you on a journey from science to evolutionary thought. How you refuel your business and create an energy ecosystem takes you into the realm of physics, spirituality, neurology, and Eastern philosophy. Your business is a human being disguised as the Empire State Building. Just like a person, your business as a whole is suffering from the human energy crisis and needs to be refueled in order to perform with ease. Just like a person, your business has its own internal energy centers that Eastern medicine calls a chakra system—centers that circulate energy throughout your business. And just like a person, your business chakras get clogged, toxic, and stagnant with unhealthy emotion and thought that wreaks havoc on performance. Get your business chakras cleared and start circulating healthy energy throughout the business, and you automatically energize your people, ignite action, and drive profits.

To accomplish this, your business must become a fully functional energy ecosystem that operates with the Eight Principles of Business. The Eight Principles of Business align directly with your business chakra system. In the pages to come, you'll be given a step-by-step roadmap for building your ecosystem, and you'll learn how to apply the following Eight Principles of Business to attract exactly what you want: energy, action, and profits.

Principle #1: Functional leaders drive profits.

Leader functionality is the key to unleashing human energy and driving profits. Sitting at the crown chakra of your business, leadership energy spills over into all aspects of the business, creating an environment that either fuels productive energy or breeds exhaustion.

Principle #2: Vision and purpose ignite forward momentum.

Vision and purpose give people inside your business the guidance and wisdom to move forward. As the third eye chakra of your business, vision and purpose create clear thinking and the focus necessary to attain goals and aspirations.

Principle #3: Truth and clarity motivate action.

Internal communication is a delicate balance between silence and words for the benefit of motivation. Internal communication lives within the throat chakra of your business, and it's within this energy center that the business needs to convey responsibility and decisions with clarity and truth.

Principle #4: People are driven to live out a purpose.

"I want to spread my wings and fly, be part of something greater than myself, and feel like I'm living my purpose." This is the voice of Principle #4. Sitting within the thymus chakra of your business, creating opportunity for people to become engaged in the business on their terms drives this energy center.

Principle #5: Freedom turns ideas and vision into reality.

Ideas and vision are attained through attitude—also called an internal brand. Sitting at the heart chakra, the right business attitude is fueled by compassion, trust, and freedom. When a business has a healthy attitude there's nothing it can't accomplish.

Principle #6: Creative expression fuels change and growth.

Change and growth are propelled forward by environment. A healthy aesthetic and cultural environment breeds confidence in individuality, intellect, and common sense. Sitting at the solar plexus chakra of the business, it is the environment that gives people permission, protection, and freedom to move the business forward.

Principle #7: Human connectivity is the source of energy.

We are all one and interconnected through energy. We feel what's going on around us, and the result is either inspiration or depletion. Sitting at the sacral chakra of the business, the home of emotion and relationship, business transparency fuels this energy center.

Principle #8: Humanity is the future.

Improving the health and well-being of humanity is the only answer to preserving a world that will continue to fuel business. The root chakra of your business is where the basic human needs of people are met, and physical safety and financial security are provided.

✳✳✳

Here's where change starts and your journey into a more profitable business begins. For thousands of years, Eastern medicine has been proving that the Eight Principles of Business refuel, manage, and maintain healthy human energy. Modern science has proven that healthy energy frequencies have the power to transform, create, and drive desired outcomes. Science has proven we *are* energy, and Eastern medicine practices have taught us *how* to manage the energy we have. The difference between now and thousands of years ago is simply the proof that science provides for the mind that doubts. My hope for you as a business leader, professional, and change agent is that you use this book as your personal advisor for creating a business that puts people at the center of decisions, process, and goals. My hope is that your mind and eyes open, and you allow yourself to embrace the new ways presented in this book to create a highly productive workplace. My hope is that you take the baton, and use the eight principles to move your business forward—mitigating toxic energy, eliminating human exhaustion, and driving profits in ways that refuel human energy and contribute to a healthier world. Let the journey begin.

Principle #1
Functional Leaders Drive Profits

We often hear people making jokes about being "dysfunctional." I've yet to meet a person who says they come from a "functional" family. Does the Brady Bunch really exist? Okay, I take that back; even they were dysfunctional. And the influx of reality TV provides a whole new model of dysfunctional being played out for future generations. Watching dysfunctional behavior on our favorite shows may be a great form of entertainment, but when the energy of a dysfunctional person seeps into our personal lives, it's not so fun. In fact, it's absolutely exhausting and sucks every ounce of energy out of us. Now take it a step further. When that dysfunctional person is the leader who controls our everyday work-life, we become absolutely miserable—here comes the energetic green slime from the Introduction again. On the flip side, when we have a leader who is inspiring and leads from a place of integrity, we become energetically refueled and healthy simply by her presence. A business is only as healthy as the people who comprise it, regardless of tools or process.

To energize your people, ignite action, and drive profits, all you have to do is create functional leaders who lead from a place of high character—putting healthy energy right back into the business. Voilá! Everything is fixed! Easier said than done, right? Dysfunctional behavior is a leadership epidemic throughout the world. I get it. And that's the exact reason why leadership functionality is Principle #1. If your business is to have any hope for successfully refueling human energy and driving future profits, you have to make the energetic health of your leaders the number-one priority of your business. You have to turn dysfunctional leadership behavior into functional leadership behavior driven by high-character values. And it's not an all-or-nothing game—every incremental step by a leader is critical to attaining healthy energy in your business.

In January 2013, Fred Kiel, cofounder of KRW International, a leadership and team development company, presented his research in a TED Talk, proving that character matters in leadership, and high-character leaders achieve three times more than low-character leaders when it comes to ROA (return on asset) and employee engagement. The performance swing went from -0.57 percent in losses due to low-character leadership, to 8.39-percent gains from high-character leaders. The trend was consistent in both ROA and employee engagement levels. The study defined high-character leaders as having high integrity, responsibility, forgiveness, and compassion.

Kiel's study was conducted throughout six years, on 100 CEOs from Fortune 500 and 1,000 companies, and sampled more than 8,000 employee observations—a ton of data that produced undeniable hard facts. Wake up, Corporate America! The question is no longer, *Does character matter?* The question now is, *How do we make sure that high-character leaders are running the businesses that impact humanity and our world?* The study also unearthed a remarkable data point: Character can be taught.

In June 2010, Brene Brown revealed her research findings on vulnerability. Brown's six-year study yielded thousands of observation samples from people all over the world. Her research concluded that allowing ourselves to be vulnerable is the only way a human being will ever feel joy, love, purpose, and an intrinsic sense of "I am enough. I am worthy." In the study, vulnerability is defined as the willingness to do something without a guaranteed result, having the courage to be imperfect, having the ability to be kind to ourselves first, and believing that the things that make you most susceptible and weak to the world are what make you most beautiful. The key to joy, love, and purpose *is* vulnerability.

Brown revealed that the missing component in our society today is our ability to be vulnerable. She also proved that vulnerability is a huge challenge in our society, a society that has been named the most in-debt, obese, medicated, and addicted in U.S. history—a society where shame and fear run rabid. As a means of survival and protection from fear and shame, our society has become an expert in denial. We pretend things that are uncertain are, in fact, certain; we pretend we are what we're not; we put ourselves on a conquest to perfect our existence. All the while, at the core of our human nature, we want to be vulnerable and feel connected—that's why we are here.

So here's the connection between Kiel's study on leadership character and Brown's study on vulnerability, and why both studies are critical to *Principle #1: Functional leaders drive profits.* The only way you can have a healthy energy ecosystem in your business is by having functional leaders who lead from a place of high character. Yes, leadership character can be taught, but you can't learn character without allowing yourself to be vulnerable. Until you allow yourself to be vulnerable as a leader, you will forever remain in a state of dysfunction, void of the true character that is proven to get business results. Now here's the beauty: You can't argue the data. High-character leaders get results, three times the return on assets of low-character leaders. Whom do you think employees want to work for? Whom do you think investors want running the business? And what kind of leader do you think will energize people, ignite action, drive profits, and move our world forward? If you said *functional leaders*, you are correct.

We learned in the Introduction that we're all energetically interconnected. Every person is impacted by the energy frequencies produced by the emotions and thoughts of everyone else in the business. If the energy being released into the business is dysfunctional, it will spread through the business like a chronic disease, leaving people exhausted, unproductive, overworked, and unhealthy. As the disease worsens, even the people who are intentionally trying to put healthy energy into the business become infected. Ultimately, the people who are aware of the dysfunctional energy, and who want to surround themselves with healthy energy, *will* leave the business in pursuit of a healthier environment. As time goes on, people inside the infected business will have to put on biohazard suits made from fear and shame. Forget about character and vulnerability, because the business becomes numb and cold to the reality that human beings are the soul of the operation. Greed, arrogance, blame, and manipulation will run wild, and the business will either be forced to undergo severe cultural change or fall apart. Falling apart was a reality that hit home for one of the companies being run by a low-character leader in Kiel's study.

Here's another truth: People who work for a business automatically give power to those leading the business. This "giving of power" has a great deal to do with the root chakra, our body's energy center that houses our emotions regarding finances, security, and safety— our basic human needs. In an energetically healthy environment where leaders understand they have a responsibility to take care of themselves, to exercise high character, and to show vulnerability, this can be a great thing. We've all experienced a leader who emanates healthy energy. These are the leaders who are great mentors, who inspire employees, and who get results. These are the leaders everyone wants to work for. However, if the business breeds unhealthy leadership energy, giving leaders automatic power is detrimental to everyone involved. Giving power to dysfunctional leaders will infect the business with chronic energetic illness, thereby harming everyone in the business while harming themselves.

It's amazing to me how many dysfunctional leaders tell me, "We have it completely under control. Our senior leaders have put together a solid culture or leadership development plan that will fix our issues. The ideas you're presenting are way too progressive for our leaders." Here's the deal: Businesses today need progressive ideas, evolutionary thought, and a new approach to "fixing" leadership and culture issues. If you want people to perform, consumers to keep buying, and profits to be driven into the future, you have to start by taking a chance and introducing business practices that may be outside your comfort zone and your "normal." Most business leaders realize this when they are able to assess the business in a less personal, less threatening way.

It all comes down to one thing: improving the energy inside your business. The children's movie *Monsters, Inc.* sends this message home by reminding us that energy from a happy laugh is much more powerful, contagious, and sustainable than energy from a fearful scream. And everyone always feels good after the laugh. The energy from functional leaders gives the business freedom to keep laughing.

The Toxic Leadership Quiz

If you're still wondering, "Does my business really need help with energy, or are these just outrageous claims?" here's a little quiz that will tell you if your business is suffering from toxic leadership energy. Simply answer True or False to the following statements. When you respond to the statements, you can either think about one area of your business or the business as a whole.

_____   Leaders are more focused on C-suite, divisional, or owner direction than people.

_____   Leaders are being overtaken by perceived loss of power, heightened level of responsibility, or directional "unknowns."

_____   Leaders are showing their "worst" frequently or more than usual.

_____   Leaders have become frozen by politics, and/or are allowing politics to drive decisions even when better options exist.

_____   People are leaving the business or thinking about it.

_____   Engagement scores are, at a minimum, satisfactory, or decreasing, and these scores are being accepted due to other priorities within the business.

_____   Employee retention is low overall, or significant gaps in particular areas of the business are evident.

_____   People have a tendency to blame others and make excuses for their mistakes rather than accept ownership and take responsibility.

_____   People feel that they can't make any decisions without receiving specific approval from management prior to doing simple tasks or taking care of customers.

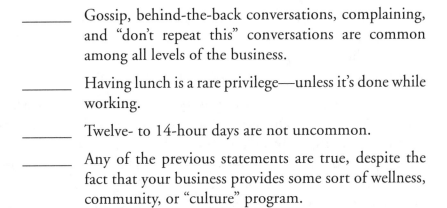

_____ Gossip, behind-the-back conversations, complaining, and "don't repeat this" conversations are common among all levels of the business.

_____ Having lunch is a rare privilege—unless it's done while working.

_____ Twelve- to 14-hour days are not uncommon.

_____ Any of the previous statements are true, despite the fact that your business provides some sort of wellness, community, or "culture" program.

Answering "True" to any of these questions is a red flag that the leaders running your business need help detoxifying, balancing, and managing their personal energy—for the sake of their own health and well-being, and for the health and well-being of employees. If you answered "False" to all of the statements, congrats! But if you're like most businesses, you answered "True" to at least one, if not all of the statements. Answering "True" to five or more statements indicates your business has energetic cancer, and the leaders running the business are putting your business at risk for a slow, miserable death. Remember the river analogy from the Introduction? We are all interconnected by energy, and if your leaders aren't functional, they're dumping green energetic slime into the river and it's killing the fish!

That being said, most people don't wake up in the morning thinking, "I want to be a complete a-hole today, and put energy into the world that harms other people. Oh, and by 5 p.m. I want to make sure I piss off at least five people...let's make that 10." On the contrary, most people want to do good things for our world, be part of something great, and experience joy, love, and purpose. They want to have a good, healthy life filled with connection, and to know they helped someone else feel good along the way. We have a world filled with good people. Truly. In fact, in nearly two decades of one-on-one interactions with business professionals, I have yet to meet someone who hasn't told me, "I want to be seen as a good person, a person who adds value, and a leader whom others look up to." When it comes right down to it, even if they can't find the words to tell you, most leaders want to be functional.

Sometimes the rest of the business forgets that its leaders are human beings, just as many leaders forget that it's people who are running the business. To bring the message home, in the following list are examples of everyday leaders whose thoughts and emotions are spilling over into all areas of the business. These leaders, similar to yours, are exhausted and desperately want to feel good again. They want to be their best selves. They want to be functional leaders who operate from a place of character. All of these leaders have experienced the typical coaching and workshops—they've drunk the Kool-Aid of success. Yet they're still filled with sabotaging thoughts and emotions that pour unhealthy energy into the business.

* Sarah sits in rush-hour traffic frantically pulling the phone out of her purse to text her next appointment, her son's nanny, and her husband to let them know that the day got away from her—she's late, again. Filled with anxiety and the all-too-familiar feeling of failure and shame, she replays in her mind everything she did wrong today, what she does wrong every day. The thoughts play like a broken record.

* Kerry sits at her desk, closes her eyes, and becomes sick to her stomach from a feeling of inadequacy. Working 12, sometimes 14 hours a day, eating lunch at her desk if she gets a chance, all while immersed in thoughts that she's a terrible mother and wife. She desperately wants "me" time, but that doesn't fit into the schedule of success. She forces herself to the next meeting, always maintaining her professional "I'm fine" persona.

* Walking through the doors of the corporate office, Tom wonders why he keeps going. He has the money, authority, status, and respect. He's making it, conquering the mountain

of success. He seems to have it all. But inside, he's miserable, exhausted, and overcome by the feeling that he'll lose everything with one wrong move—one bad decision away from failure. One day they might all find out he has no idea what the hell he's doing.

✴ Entering yet another meeting, Erin wonders why they even want her there. Does she add value? Do they really think she's deserving of her position? Lost. Not really knowing where she's going, why she's there, what they want from her. Nervous. Anxious. Tired. Maybe it's she who doesn't want to be there. She knows she's trapped in this existence due to personal issues that feel completely out of her control. All in a day's work.

✴ Sunday morning, Dan sits at his desk at home, rubbing his head in an effort to focus, to get it together, summon enough energy to get all the work done that he needs to finish before the morning—work that, if he doesn't finish, will turn his week into another brutal mess. He's trying to breathe while the thoughts of giving up keep surfacing. "Is this what I really want from life? God, what happened to me?"

Energy Work

Businesses need to take a more progressive approach to leadership development. Humanity needs businesses to have the courage to try something new, and be early adopters in the world of health and wellness by addressing what every human being is made of: energy. It's time to expand your mind and be courageous by moving forward with a different approach to getting your business leaders healthy and productive.

Wellness is a $1.3 trillion industry, and still the health of adults continues to decrease. Businesses globally are being impacted, faced with workplace stress, obesity, and chronic disease among employees. Our nation continues to put forth "get healthy" initiatives, corporations continue providing leadership coaching and traditional wellness programs, yet humanity gets unhealthier by the minute. As you can see from the individual leaders in the earlier examples, your leaders are likely no exception. They are in desperate need of an alternative way to get healthy from the inside out. They want to put good, healthy energy back into the business, but until they are energetically healthy and holistically functional, their energy will continue to be harmful to your business and everyone in it.

The only way to get your leaders energetically healthy is by healing the energy they have, replenishing their system with healthy energy, and teaching them how to manage and protect their personal energy. This can be done easily through the practice of energy work. Energy work influences the flow of energy though our bodies, positively impacting our thoughts, emotions, and actions. The regular practice of energy work improves personal energy flow, reduces exhaustion, increases productivity, and allows us to be vulnerable—creating the opportunity to experience transformative growth and begin living a high-character life.

During an energy work session, each energy center, or chakra, within our body is cleared and replenished, which impacts our thoughts, emotions, and actions. When energy is flowing smoothly through each chakra, we're able to make better decisions, be vulnerable, show character that adds value, and live our personal lives with a sense of wellbeing. The practice of energy work, when guided by a trained practitioner, addresses our physical and emotional needs. During energy work sessions, practitioners ask questions associated with energy blockages to uncover what's at the core of dysfunctional behavior, and they facilitate a path of self-discovery. The practice of energy work in business accelerates transformative change and growth in leaders. When you're looking for a practitioner for your business, it's vital to partner with an energetic practitioner who can effortlessly bridge the world of business and the world of energy. An extraordinary leader in this emerging field is Jeanine Thompson, a psychotherapist, former Fortune 50 executive, and energy worker. A Business Energy Expert like Jeanine can lead the way to quantum shifts that not only refuel your leaders, but ignite productivity, prosperity, and the overall health of your business. These energy practitioners exist. You need to find one for your leaders! Your leaders aren't broken; they just need to be energetically refueled so they can begin looking at life with a sense of inspiration again. That inspiration will carry over into the business and create a contagious sense of optimism and drive among everyone.

Balancing the chakra system within each of your leaders is the first step in turning your business into an energy ecosystem that energizes people, ignites action, and drives profits. Following are detailed descriptions of the thoughts, emotions, and actions each chakra influences, and how it relates to functional leadership and your business.

The Crown Chakra

The crown chakra is located right above your head. With your crown chakra in balance, you fully understand your meaning and purpose in the world, and you feel supported and confident in living your purpose. You can see the bigger picture without emotion or attachment, but with a sense of complete fulfillment and peace beyond the material world.

How balancing the crown chakra impacts your business: Ted is the VP of Marketing for a mid-sized manufacturing company. Colleagues enjoy working with him on projects and strategy because he's always mentally present. When other people are talking, he's actually listening, looking into the eyes of the person speaking, and asking clarifying questions without judgment or the pursuit of ammunition for his response. During strategy meetings, Ted never has an agenda that weighs heavily in the room, eroding overall trust. He has the innate ability to keep his eye on the vision of the business, while inspiring others to do the same. He draws from the past to make decisions only if it's directly relevant as an objective "lesson learned" or "best practice" that deserves to be carried forward into the present.

Ted has become the leader whom new managers want to learn from and be around. His energy is healthy and people feel confident and secure in his presence. He gives off a presence that communicates, "Anything is possible. It just is." Not only is Ted a smart businessman with a proven track record of top-performing results in dire circumstances, but his attitude of possibility also seems to make things happen automatically. He's most admired by his colleagues for taking ownership, and being aware of his own behavior when it gets off track, always willing to try new approaches to working with others. Ted is a high-character leader.

The Third Eye Chakra

Located at the center of your forehead. Your third eye chakra is the home of your inner vision, guidance, and wisdom. When your third eye chakra is balanced, you listen to your intuition, have the high mental ability to differentiate between reality and emotion, and are clear-thinking and focused. You trust and are able to distinguish between sabotaging thoughts and insight (intuition).

How balancing the third eye chakra impacts your business: Lisa is the business owner of an up-and-coming technology firm. Lisa is known among her peers as a smart and witty businesswoman who's willing to take risks and who has the ability to turn business ventures into gold. When asked how she ultimately makes her business decisions, her response is always, "I listen to my gut and trust my instincts." Because she trusts her intuition, she's a great judge of character, and she gives people who work for her the freedom to take care of the business in their own unique way—without pointing fingers or passing blame if things go wrong. Everyone in the company admires Lisa, which is a direct reason why she has maintained a 5-percent attrition rate in an industry that has rapid turnover. People in her company perform at higher levels in comparison to the competition because they feel protected and free to do so. Lisa is a high-character leader.

The Throat Chakra

Located at your throat, your throat chakra fuels your communication, ability to make yourself heard, and ease in speaking your own truth. When balanced, you express your ideas openly and with conviction, and you convey responsibility and decisions with clarity, and truth without hesitation or fear of others' thoughts and opinions. You clearly communicate with complete understanding of your intent and motivation.

How balancing the throat chakra impacts your business: Sarah is the Director of Communications for a high-profile healthcare company. Sarah's role in the company has been instrumental in the last year due to recalls on two of the company's most profitable over-the-counter drugs. Sarah was able to successfully influence senior leaders to own up to the fact that the recall was due to errors in the manufacturing plant. She wrote the communication strategy that brilliantly positioned the company to consumers as an ethical brand, and fully disclosed the details of the occurrence to employees. Because of Sarah's courage and strength to stand strong in what was right, regardless of the repercussions, the business and Sarah became highly respected. Rather than hitting the job boards with disgust, employees became inspired and motivated to be working for an organization that is willing to be transparent at all costs in order to protect humanity from a potentially deadly outcome. Sarah is a high-character leader.

The Thymus Chakra

The thymus chakra is located at your upper chest. When your thymus chakra is balanced you recognize your purpose in this world.

You know how to contribute to things in this world that are greater than yourself. You are able to spread your wings and fly. You know who you are, and you embrace vulnerability and character. You acknowledge, identify, and take responsibility for the impact you have on yourself, others, and the world.

How balancing the thymus chakra impacts your business: Paul is the VP of Strategic Initiatives for a large consumer goods company. Paul was put in charge of strategic initiatives because of his ability to understand the vision of the business, and his strength in developing strategies that make sense, get results, and inspire others to perform at higher levels. Although the business has a traditional culture, prescriptive in nature, Paul's seemingly progressive and bold ideas are highly respected and supported by his colleagues. He's able to make necessary change fast in an organization that has a reputation for moving like molasses. When asked by a new business leader, "How are you able to get buy-in from everyone in the company, move your ideas forward, *and* get people to perform?" Paul's response was, "I never pitch an idea or strategy that doesn't have a strong, positive impact on people, and I make sure everyone at all levels of the business owns portions of the strategy. I tell the truth, and I always stand by my word. I believe people at all levels can feel that I have their best interests in mind, and they trust me." Paul is a functional leader.

The Heart Chakra

The heart chakra is located at your heart. When the heart chakra is in balance you feel free, yet grounded. Giving and receiving love, compassion, trust, and freedom happens naturally and openly with yourself and others. You have a balanced sense of compassion and a willingness to share. This is an important system to have in balance to bring the life you want to fruition, as it allows you to turn positive ideas and visions into reality. The heart chakra works integrally with the other chakras.

How balancing the heart chakra impacts your business:
Garrison is the manager of a mid-sized engineering firm. He's surrounded by process, technology, and analytics—all day, every day. He's the leader that needs facts and figures before making a decision. His motto: "If there's no process, it won't work. You better be able to prove it if you want to do it." He's ruthless about being on time for everything, and has incredibly high expectations when it comes to people following through on initiatives. He's a cynic by nature.

Garrison also has the highest retention rates, team performance levels, and employee engagement scores in the company. People love to work for him, and even the people who dislike process gravitate his way. Despite Garrison's rigid nature, he's always willing to teach and mentor people along the way, listen to their ideas, and encourage others to bring their ideas to fruition—and he supports them when they do. He's gained a reputation on his team for actually caring about their lives. He's the first person to ask how someone's weekend was on a Monday morning, he seeks to understand personal challenges when someone is struggling with performance, and he's always willing to share his personal life with his team regardless of the potential perception. Garrison is a functional leader.

The Solar Plexus Chakra

The solar plexus chakra is located above your navel and is the home of your "gut feeling." When your solar plexus is in balance, you have a great sense of individuality, personal value, confidence, and willpower. A balanced solar plexus fosters self-esteem, reduces anxiety, and increases common sense. It's your primary sense of self, and it's where personal boundaries are set. Your solar plexus is your key to transformation. When balanced, tremendous change and personal growth are possible.

How balancing the solar plexus chakra impacts your business: Kerry is a partner in a large accounting firm. She was recently promoted to partner after leading the company through the economic recession with a consistent 5 percent growth rate. Her management smarts earned the company an increase in margin and cost efficiencies while the competitors continued to struggle—some going out of business. Kerry earned her badge of armor in a business that prides itself on concrete logic.

Here's the twist: Unlike most leaders in her company, during the high-crisis years, Kerry turned the business over to her team. When she first realized that the company could potentially be in trouble, she called her team together on a Friday afternoon. Her opening statement was, "If this company is going to have any hope of attaining our estimated growth rates, let alone not having to lay people off in the next three years, all of you need to be part of building the plan on how we're going to move forward. I don't have all the answers. It's going to take all of us. You all have the permission and protection to be as innovative and creative as possible in developing the solutions that will get our projected results. I only have one condition: You need to make sure that you keep our people and their families top-of-mind as you surface ideas."

On that Friday afternoon, Kerry gave the people in the company freedom to express their creative ideas—no idea was too creative, too expressive, or too bold. For three months, Kerry facilitated open strategy sessions, and together everyone collectively developed the plan that would achieve results unheard of among competitors during what has now been deemed the worst economic crisis our nation has seen sense the Great Depression. Not only did Kerry receive additional ideas that helped the business, but she also got buy-in and commitment to achieving them. Kerry is a functional leader.

The Sacral Chakra

Located below your navel. The sacral chakra is the home of your relationships, and it's the emotional center of your life. It houses the emotion you have with others in your life and the sexual presence you feel you have in yourself and the world. When in balance, your sacral chakra allows you to freely express yourself clearly with creativity in all forms. When the sacral chakra is balanced, you have a sense of freedom, you're open to change, and you allow flexibility and flow in your life.

How balancing the sacral chakra impacts your business: For 10 years, Adam had been the CEO of a company that was recently acquired by a global retailer. Now he is the newly appointed VP of Operations of that global retail company.

As with most acquisitions, many of the senior leaders from the previous company were let go, demoted, or relocated, and the new CEO built a new C-suite executive team. Adam was given his new role because of his proven track record. Peers perceived Adam as being lucky that he still had a job that paid well and used his skills. Adam didn't feel so lucky as he watched two of his previous direct reports get promoted above him, "new blood" being brought into high-powered roles, and leaders whom he believed were unethical and self-serving remaining in previously held positions. As the new global C-suite was formed, backstabbing, fear, defensive attacks, and power struggles sent negative energy through the business. Progress seemed to stagnate, because leaders couldn't figure out how to get along and respect each other behind closed doors. Dysfunctional leadership and denial seemed to be the commonality among executive leaders, and anxiety and fear spread throughout all levels of the business because no one knew exactly what was in store for the future.

Throughout this time of turmoil, Adam's team seemed to be the only group performing, moving the business forward, and actually having fun. Peers looked at Adam in awe as they tried to figure out how he was achieving such results and keeping a focused, level head during a time of high stress and ambiguity. When someone finally asked him what was going on and how he was doing it, he simply said, "I let it go. I let go of any grudges, resentment, and hurt I felt about being demoted. I realized that if I was going to lead this company forward, I needed to focus on what mattered: the people moving the company forward. I decided to turn around and face the people on my team instead of getting sucked into unhealthy turmoil that's only going to harm the business and everyone involved. I owned up to my own past mistakes and moved on. I got my priorities straight. I just let it all go." Adam is a functional leader.

The Root Chakra

The root chakra is located at your base organs. When your root chakra is open and clear, you feel financially secure, physically safe, stable, and present; not flakey, or as though you're floating through life. The root chakra strengthens your ability to carry on conversations with concentration in the moment, and manage basic details of your physical existence such as paying bills and keeping your schedule straight.

How balancing the root chakra impacts your business: Andrew is the owner of a consumer electronics company. He has a reputation for meeting deadlines, keeping promises, being consistently on time, and always exceeding expectations by keeping his word and doing everything he can to make sure the people involved in the business are taken care of. Andrew clearly understands that if the people running the business are taken care of personally, then performance expectations will be met and the customer will always benefit.

As the owner of the business, he intentionally set up a board of advisors designed to keep himself in check and accountable for making solid business decisions. Last year, Andrew took the board of advisors one step further and created a humanitarian council.

The council includes the executive leadership team and employees from various levels of the business—all departments and levels are represented. The intent of the council is twofold: to ensure all business decisions serve the employees and leave the world a better place, and to develop humanitarian efforts outside business-as-usual activities that serve the employees. The council's first initiative included an onsite clinic that provided both alternative and traditional medical care for employees. Andrew even used his own money to build the clinic.

When employees are asked about Andrew's leadership ability, they respond by saying, "He takes care of us, and it's clear that he's trying to leave this world a better place. His drive makes us want to work harder, take care of the customers better, and be more like him." Andrew is a functional leader.

High-Character Values

When a leader's chakra system is in balance, she is able to model and live high-character values—a significant element of functional leadership. The Eight Principles of Business take Kiel's character study forward by adding an additional four values: mindful awareness, freedom, truth, and creative expression. Living each of the eight values shows leader maturity. As leader functionality increases, high-character values become more evident in the leader's day-to-day actions. When leaders feel exhausted, zapped of energy, and filled with toxic energy, they show their worst selves, and character goes out the window. As the energy within us becomes healthy, living high-character values becomes easy. The health of our energy and our ability to live high-character values go hand in hand. These are the eight high-character values you want expressed by your leaders:

1. **Mindful Awareness:** Mindful awareness is being present—always. It's the ability to look into the future and reflect on the

past without getting trapped in either place. It's consciousness of your actions and emotions. Living in a state of mindfulness allows you to identify whether you are living each of the eight character values. You have the ability to correct your actions and get back into alignment with living the high-character values.

2. **Freedom:** Freedom drives revenue by giving everyone in the business the permission and protection to address challenges, manage initiatives, and develop strategies in their own unique way. When leaders exhibit the value of freedom, they trust everyone involved, and their need for providing constant oversight is removed.

3. **Truth:** Truth drives mobility in both people and the business. When leaders are transparent in all accounts and without exception, people are inspired and motivated to help move the business forward, and they have a desire to move into more significant roles in support of the business. Living the value of truth negates denial; excuses dissipate, and ownership for mistakes becomes obvious. "I'm honored to work for such business or such leader" is the benchmark statement when a leader lives the value of truth.

4. **Integrity:** Integrity drives trust by acting consistently with principles, values, and beliefs, telling the truth, standing up for what is right, and keeping promises. Integrity takes courage and fearless conviction—especially if the business as a whole does not operate with integrity. When a leader lives integrity, he ensures the business operates with truth and what is right for humanity by first putting the people who work for the business at the center of his decisions, without wavering.

5. **Compassion:** Compassion heightens engagement and talent retention. Compassion is about genuinely empathizing with others, and showing sympathy with authenticity. Compassion breeds trust, respect, and loyalty throughout the business, and shows everyone that the business has heart. When leaders

have compassion, it's evident that they care about how the business impacts people and communities.

6. **Creative Expression:** Creative expression drives margins and elevates cost efficiencies. When people feel they have truly been given the freedom to express themselves openly, ideas and innovation flow easily through the business. Change becomes more fluid and effective, because people take ownership for their ideas and the possibilities their ideas have created for others.

7. **Forgiveness:** Forgiveness fuels innovation and is the genuine act of letting go of one's own mistakes, as well as those of others. Forgiveness is the most challenging of all the values due to our human tendency to hold on to grudges, hang on to past resentment, dwell on hurt, and harbor shame associated with perceived failure. The key to living the value of forgiveness is to forgive yourself first—the rest becomes that much easier.

8. **Responsibility:** A direct partner of truth, responsibility is about inspiring and driving action by taking ownership for personal choices, admitting mistakes and failures, embracing the responsibility for serving others, and leaving the world a better place. When leaders live the value of responsibility, deadlines are met, promises are kept, and the overall performance of the business improves.

The Process: Creating Functional Leaders

Now it's time to start turning your business into an energy ecosystem that energizes people, ignites action, and drives profits. Leadership sits at the crown chakra of your business, and it becomes healthy when you apply (1) accountability, (2) leadership energy work, and (3) a solid mentor program.

1. Accountability

The business needs to hold all its leaders accountable to living high-character values, and clearly communicate the expectation that all leaders become functional. This means the review process, bonus structure, stock options, and any other benefit that has a direct tie to monetary compensation only goes to high-character leaders—period! Yes, other performance metrics are also important, but how a leader lives high-character values on a daily basis must hold a 50-percent review weight at minimum. This is called the Character Value Score (CVS). The CVS is a cumulative result of employee and peer observation surveys, engagement survey results, and employee retention. As you've learned so far, it's high-character leaders who get results—three times more than low-character leaders. If the business is serious about energizing people, igniting action, and driving profits, then the business needs to get serious about functional leadership. And, given the current state of our society and the world of business, if you are to have any hope of making change in the leadership arena, you need to hit the pain point, the security blanket, the and elephant in the room: money.

2. Leadership Energy Work

The second step in the process is all about getting your leaders healthy and functional from the inside out. Each leader running your business needs to receive one 90-minute energy work session every week for the first 90 days, and every two weeks thereafter. During each session, leaders are guided through a process of releasing and letting go of baggage, and addressing roadblocks that prevent them from attaining functionality. They are left with fresh perspective, insight, and a clear direction for how to move forward. Again, it's critical that the business partner with a trained practitioner who understands business energetics. These practitioners exist—find one! It will be the best investment you've ever made for yourself and your business.

3. A Solid Mentor Program

The third step in turning your business into an energy ecosystem is a mentor program for your leaders. This is *not* leadership coaching. Mentoring is about building a trusted relationship with someone further along the functionality curve than you. A leader can look to this person for advice, guidance, and an example of what *great* looks like in regard to living out high-character values. The business needs to create a structured program that makes it easy for leaders to get involved and find a mentor. Additionally, it needs to be clear to all leaders in your business that the mentor program is *not optional*. Your high-functional leaders automatically become mentors once they have attained a consistent state of functional leadership—identified by the CVS.

The mentor program needs to be a cornerstone of your business. If the business does not currently have functional leaders, or it is not large enough to support a mentor program, you need to partner with other businesses or seek out functional leaders in your network. I've never met a functional leader who has turned down an opportunity to be a mentor—it doesn't happen, because functional leaders have a strong desire to help and serve other leaders.

✳✳✳

You are now well on your way toward turning your business into a healthy energy ecosystem that drives profits. The final message is simple: The energetic health of your leaders is the most important priority of your business and is critical to its financial success. It doesn't matter if you're the CEO of a billion-dollar company or the owner of an ice cream shop—get functional; your business depends on it.

Chapter Highlights

* **Functional leaders drive profits.**

* Leader functionality is the key to unleashing healthy human energy and driving profits. Sitting at the crown chakra of your business, leadership energy spills over into all aspects of the business, creating an environment that either fuels productive energy or breeds exhaustion.

* High-character leaders achieve three times more than low-character leaders when it comes to ROA (return on asset) and employee engagement.

* Character can be taught.

* The key to joy, love, and purpose is vulnerability. Without vulnerability, a person will remain in misery. A person must be vulnerable in order to learn character.

* Before your business can have an energetically healthy crown chakra, each individual leader has to have a healthy chakra system.

* When a leader's chakra system is in balance, she is able to model the way to live high-character values—a significant element of functional leadership.

* The only way to get your leaders energetically healthy is to heal the energy they have, replenish their system with healthy energy, and teach them how to manage and protect their personal energy through energy work.

* There are three steps in turning your business into a healthy energy ecosystem: (1) Integrate the CVS into annual reviews with a direct impact to compensation. (2) Make energy work a regular component of leadership development. (3) Create a systematic mentor program that connects leaders to high-character role models.

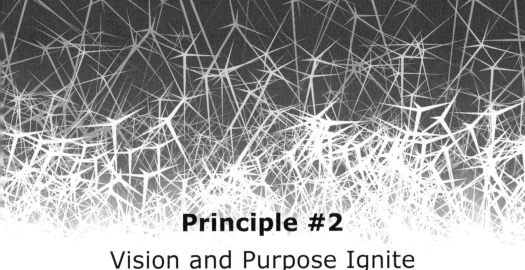

Principle #2

Vision and Purpose Ignite Forward Momentum

Energy is dynamic and always moving. The energy within us is in a constant state of interaction with everything else in our environment, and whatever frequency you put out into the world will be the reality you experience. When people are filled with anxiety and frustration because they have no idea where their business is going, their thoughts and emotions create unhealthy energy. The result is an energy-depleted work environment. Remember the butterfly effect? Your energy frequencies have the ability to cause great turmoil or tremendous outcomes. Tremendous outcomes happen when healthy energy circulates throughout the business. Healthy energy is possible when people's thoughts become clear and focused, and their emotions become calm. No one can get to a state of calm while driving and searching for directions at the same time. If the business wants the clear-headed thinking that generates healthy energy, then the business needs to clearly define where it's going, why it's going there, and how it's planning to get there.

Principle #2 is all about the strength of vision and purpose—the power of intent. It's the third eye chakra of your business, and it gives people the guidance and wisdom to move forward. It creates clear thinking and focus, a state of mind that's absolutely necessary if a business wants to reach its aspirations. Vision and purpose have the ability to circulate healthy energy throughout the business because when people are aligned and know where they're going, they can work smarter, not harder.

A clearly defined vision and purpose reduces anxiety. It eliminates self-sabotaging thoughts and emotions that people drown in when they're swimming in a pool of the unknown. It's amazing: Let people know exactly where the business is going and how to get there, and the business has happy people. But keep everything a secret, behind closed doors, and only available to management, or just don't bother figuring out the vision and purpose at all, and the business automatically has ulcers everywhere. Here we go again—your business just got energetically slimed.

Imagine this: You're in your car at 10 a.m. and you have a meeting in 30 minutes. No worries. You have your phone, and the GPS is on. All good. You're actually kind of excited for the meeting because it's taking place at the brand new Innovation Building your company built this year, and you're going to get the chance to meet Bob, the executive who's spearheading the Innovation for Humanity initiative your company is launching next year. Next week, you're interviewing to be one of the leaders heading up the initiative. Today is the opportunity you've been waiting for to make a great first impression with Bob. A very exciting day. It all starts in 30 minutes!

Coffee and cell phone in hand (you only brought one of your phones with you this time), you're off and driving. It's a beautiful day. You're listening to U2 on the radio. The sky is blue. And a nice breeze is coming through the windows. You are relaxed.

All of sudden your phone starts beeping. You look down and notice that the GPS isn't working. You have no idea how to get to the Innovation Building. You grab the phone to call the home office and get directions, but you only have one bar and service keeps going in and out. You check the printout of the meeting invite and no directions are included. You say out loud, "What the hell! Why is this happening right now? There is no reason why I should only have one bar; the sky is perfectly clear!" In that moment, you come to a small traffic jam. All the cars are waiting for a traffic light that appears to be permanently red. Your heart starts beating faster, and you begin feeling sick to your stomach. The meeting is starting in 15 minutes.

Up ahead there's an exit for Interstate 90 East and West. You remember someone at the office saying that the Innovation Building is off of Interstate 90. You say, "Damn it! Do I go east or west, east or west, east or west?" You choose east, and merge onto I-90.

As you head down 1-90 East you remember that Sarah, one of your coworkers, handed you directions to the Innovation Building last week. You stuffed the directions in your workbag. "Yes! Thank God for Sarah!" While driving, you reach in the back seat for your bag, and at the same time your coffee spills all over your lap. "Crap! Seriously, is this really happening right now?" You manage to get the directions...only to find that you needed to take I-90 West. You look at the clock, and the meeting now starts in two minutes. Frantically, you take the next exit, turn around, and get on I-90 heading west.

You are now 15 minutes late for the meeting, sweating profusely, coffee on your pants, and your heart is beating a million miles a minute. You are full of anxiety, embarrassment, and fear that you're now going to make a horrible first impression with Bob. You're convinced that there is no way you will ever get the new leadership role. You start talking yourself off the cliff. "Calm down. Relax. It's going to be okay. Breathe. Breathe. Breathe." You collect yourself. As you arrive at the Innovation Building, you notice that you now have a full five bars on your cell phone. You say under your breath, "Well that's helpful...*not.*"

When you walk into the conference room of the Innovation Building, no one is there. The room is completely empty. "What?" You head to the front desk and ask the woman where everyone is. The woman, in a very chipper voice, says, "Oh, that meeting is tomorrow morning at 10:30 a.m. Didn't they tell you it changed?" You just stare at her with a blank look. "Tomorrow? No, I didn't know."

Exhausted, and completely confused, you walk back to your car. You look at the schedule on your phone to make sure you're not crazy. Your calendar confirms that the meeting was today at 10:30 a.m. Okay, you're not crazy.

When you get back to the office, you head right to the Admin. "What happened?" The Admin simply says, "Oh, it was a last-minute change. Didn't anyone tell you? We must have forgotten to add you to the new communication list. Oops. Oh well, we'll get you on the list next time."

After all this, you have no motivation to work or accomplish anything, and your pants still have coffee on them. You're tired. What you really want to do is just go home and veg. You begrudgingly sit at your desk and start reading through 10 critical e-mails. You take a deep breath and decide that you'll suck it up and get through your day on autopilot.

We've all experienced a morning similar to this. Even the most organized of people find themselves in high-stress situations due to others' lack of direction. Spin it however you want—you should have left earlier; you should have brought two phones (because that's helpful); you should have gone old school and printed out the directions before you left; you should have remembered that Sarah gave you the directions last week; and you should have checked with the Admin before you left to make sure nothing had changed—just in case. Well, I have a novel "should have" for you: The business should have clearly communicated the change, made sure everyone was crystal clear on the new message, and included directions in the meeting invite. That might have been helpful.

We can all find humor in the story, but it's not so funny when you realize it's a metaphor for your business. The "meeting" is the vision of your business. "Meeting Bob, and landing the new leadership role" is the purpose of your business. And the chaos of "getting directions and getting there on time" is how most people feel as they are desperately trying to figure out what the leaders running the business actually want. Most people have it even worse; our story assumes that the business actually *has* a high-level vision and purpose, when that's not usually the case.

Vision and purpose, for your business, is like a harbor's lighthouse on a stormy night. The purpose is clear: Get the ships safely to the harbor. The lighthouse achieves this purpose by having one bright light that shines out to sea, guiding all of the ships toward it. If the lighthouse had no light, the ships would have no idea where to go and would run into rocks or crash into each other, and sink. If the lighthouse had multiple lights shining all at one time the same thing would happen. Instead, the lighthouse engineer understands that in order to get all the ships to their destination, there needs to be one bright, undeniable light that guides each ship to shore.

Similarly, a business needs to have a clear purpose for why it exists, and one bright light that brings people toward the ultimate destination. Some businesses try to get away with only having a purpose, saying, "Our purpose is strong enough to move the business forward. All people need to know is why they're here." Some businesses try to get away with only having a vision, saying,

"Knowing the end destination is what motivates and inspires movement. That's all we need." The reality is that a business needs both. People need to be confident that they know why the business exists, and they need to be able to trust that the light you're shining will get them to the right destination.

When your business doesn't have a clear vision and purpose, it becomes disjointed. Individual work silos pop up everywhere as a survival technique. Each work silo lives by the same silent manta: "If the business leaders can't figure out an actual vision and purpose, we're just going to make one up." And people do. This creates redundant work, frustration due to projects going nowhere, political nightmares, and a significant loss of human energy.

Picture a field of giant windmills that are creating enough power to sustain two cities. One side of the field fuels the city of Stony Creek. All the windmills on the Stony Creek side are beautifully aligned, facing in the same direction in order to be propelled by the wind and produce enough power for the city. Stony Creek also created windmill groups—evenly placed windmills that work together, making sure the city has constant power no matter where the wind is coming from. Looking at the field, the windmills seem to be propelled effortlessly forward, together, as the wind blows. The city of Stony Creek prides itself on how well the windmill field came together. The new power source reduced city costs and allowed the city of Stony Creek to renovate its downtown—an effort that resulted in more business, more jobs, and a healthier environment.

On the other side of the field are the windmills that power the city of Garrisburg, all facing in a different direction—no groups, no alignment. Some of them are similar, but none of them are facing the exact same direction as another. With every gust of wind some windmills move, some don't. Some of the windmills appear to be working very hard, and at the same time, some windmills are not working at all. When a big gust of wind comes along, the windmills that do move go into overdrive, and their gears burn out. When this happens the city loses power—a costly occurrence for the city. City officials can't figure out why things are going so terribly wrong. They hired very smart people to build the windmills. Everywhere you go in the city you hear people saying, "You would think they could figure out how to make sure the windmills produce power and don't break! Who's running the show anyway?"

Of course we're not just talking about windmills; we're talking about business. The analogy is simple: Get everyone in the business *clearly* understanding what direction your business needs to move, and magic happens! Just like Stony Creek, you get more customers buying, and you create more jobs and a healthier work environment. Or, you can choose to be Garrisburg and live with constant power outages, profit loss, and employees who tell everyone, including customers, that you have no clue how to run the joint. Seems like the choice is easy. Bottom line: figure out where you're going, why you're going there, and how it's going to happen. Then clearly communicate it to everyone.

Now, before you run into the office and schedule a weekend retreat for your leaders, an off-site strategy session, or a top-secret senior management meeting to figure out your vision and purpose—STOP! Seriously, stop the madness. Here's the reality, and the "little" nuance to this whole vision and purpose thing: Your leadership team can come up with a brilliant vision, purpose, and strategy, and you can spend months crafting just the right language for the communication memo, but if you don't have *functional leaders* delivering the message, your business *will* become Garrisburg. You'll be back to square one: energetically slimed and going nowhere fast.

The Process: Destination Mapping

Here's how functional leaders unclog and detoxify the third eye chakra of the business. The process is called Destination Mapping, and it creates a flow of healthy energy throughout your business by eliminating ambiguity. The process is easy. All you have to do is ask yourself five simple questions, share your responses clearly and consistently with everyone in the business, and inspire people by giving them guidance and freedom to reach the destination.

A Destination Map can be created by one person who owns a small business, or by a group of people who are part of a larger business. If you're choosing to facilitate a large group discussion to create your map, you need to make sure all areas and levels of the business are represented. At the end of the process, you will have a Destination Map that will ignite your business.

Question 1: What does the business want in five years?

Usually, when a business is trying to come up with a vision, the question is, *Where is the business going?* That's where the trouble begins. When I ask leaders where the business is going, I usually get a room full of blank looks until the most outspoken leader decides to get the ball rolling. Even then, the discussion often turns into a debate, and alignment is difficult, if not impossible, during the first session. However, the room usually explodes with responses when I ask the question, *What does the business **want** in five years?* That question is easy because as humans we have been programmed to answer "What do you want?" since we were children. *I want this... I want that....* Applying the question to a business is just as easy: The business wants more money. The business wants to be more efficient. The business wants its people to be happy and productive. The business wants to be fueled by healthy human energy. It's all in how we frame the question. Once you figure out what the business wants, what you have really done is created a roadmap for where the business is going. You've simply described the vision in a new way by asking the question differently.

Let's bring it back to human energy. The point of this chapter is that your business has an energy center called the third eye chakra, and the energy flow in this particular chakra is based on how the business communicates its vision and purpose. As you start thinking about what the business wants in five years, here are general guidelines that will help you craft a vision that circulates the healthy human energy that gets results:

* ✴ *Make it about more than money.* Healthy energy will not flow through your business if you state that making more money is your vision. In fact, making money your vision will actually produce an excess of harmful energy and slow your business down. In today's society, the topic of money, for most people, creates a sense of anxiety, fear, and shame. Very few people in this world, if any, are emotionally moved by a business whose vision is to make money. In fact, when money becomes the vision, people subconsciously detach themselves from the business emotionally as a means of protection. The last thing you want anyone in your business to do is emotionally detach themselves. The whole point of reading this book is to emotionally *engage* everyone back into the business. Yes, you're in business to make money, but money should always remain the outcome and not the destination.

* ✴ *Make it sustainable.* I'm talking about sustainable performance. When you determine where the business is going, you need to make sure the path to the destination can—and does—hold up for the long term. If it's not sustainable, you're going to fuel sabotaging thoughts and emotions, a lack of trust, and a tremendous resistance to change going forward with anything you do. People will make the joke that anything new in your business is just the "flavor of the month." Yes, our world is full of change, and you need to be adaptable and flexible to keep up with the competition, and in terms of strategy, that's great. But when it comes to the vision and purpose of your business, you never want a moving target.

✳ ***Make it about people and the world.*** If the vision and purpose of your business lacks humanity, you can forget about refueling human energy. Healthy energy is magnified when people are contributing to something greater than themselves and taking care of our world along the way. People are driven to work for a business that cares about the world as much as they do. People want to work hard for and be loyal to a business with practices that mitigate and clean up harm to our environment. A piece of your vision and purpose needs to be about creating solutions for a better world, a healthier humanity. In the future, if your vision and purpose doesn't include humanity and the world, people will leave to work somewhere else, regardless of money, and customers will stop buying your products and services.

✳ ***Make it bold but attainable.*** People are energized by a bold business vision and purpose. Jim Collins, in his book *Good to Great*, said it best when he introduced the world to the BHAG—Big Hairy Audacious Goals. You want your vision and purpose to be big, but make sure it's still attainable. It doesn't matter how aspirational and inspiring your vision and purpose is; if the destination seems too far out of reach, people will become demotivated and filled with sabotaging thoughts and emotions that create unhealthy energy for the business. Another word of caution: A big piece of attainability is whether leaders are able to "walk the talk." If you're not 100-percent confident that your leaders can live up to a vision and purpose that includes taking care of humanity, keeping a sustainable focus, and making the destination about more than money, go back to Chapter 1. You can't move forward if your leaders aren't functional. No matter how attainable the vision, it will never be reached if people have to move through toxic leadership energy to get there.

✳ ***Keep it simple.*** I get a kick out of paragraph-long vision statements that are filled with "corporate speak." When you develop your vision, use real language that everyone understands. Seriously, throw out the binder of terms you had to create because of made-up business jargon. If the fancy words you use are not technical terms having to do with products and services, get rid of them. I'm talking about terms like *foundational excellence, cultural efficiencies, communicative leadership,* and *operational effectiveness.* When people outside of management see "corporate speak" here's what they say when you're not looking: "What the hell does that mean? What do they want me to do? Cultural what? Excellent what? Yeah, I have no idea. I'm just going to keep doing what I always do until someone says something." If it's not simple, it gets you nowhere fast.

Question 2: Why is the destination of your business important?

This question gets to the root of purpose: why your business exists. The answer is easy if you followed the guidelines in the last section: The purpose of your business is the solution it provides to the world, what the business is fixing, making happen, or impacting. Again, similar to the vision, the purpose of your business cannot be about making more money if you are to have any hope of refueling people with healthy energy. Yes, money is important, and you may indeed have started the business because you wanted to make more of it. Great! That being said, people will not emotionally support the purpose of money—period. They'll run from it, and become mentally and physically exhausted in the process. For a purpose to ignite action toward the vision, it has to evoke positive emotion. The only way this is possible is if the purpose shows that the business wants to genuinely make the world a better place.

Question 3: In five years, what does the business look like?

No, really, what does it *physically* look like, smell like, feel like? Paint the picture in your mind. Now describe it. I get that you just came up with a fantastic five-year vision and purpose statement, but people don't care about the words on paper. People care about how the picture you paint makes them feel. They care about emotion. They care about the pleasant thoughts that enter their mind when they can see the picture you're painting as they close their eyes. They care about whether the leader who's painting the image of the future actually believes in where the business is going. They care about whether that same leader actually sees himself in the image he is painting. This is why functional leaders have to deliver the message. If the image of the future isn't vivid, if the story of where the business is going isn't filled with emotion, or if the leader who's delivering the message isn't genuine, then you have no message. People move forward when they feel emotionally compelled to move forward. People move forward when they can see and emotionally connect with the destination they're trying to reach. Leaders have to become expert storytellers.

Here's the secret to bringing everyone along the journey and becoming Stony Creek from the windmill example: You can't tell people how to get to the destination until you've painted the image of the destination. This is the number-one mistake leaders make. Businesses have an amazing vision and purpose, and then leaders jump right into telling employees *how* to get there. STOP! If you haven't vividly painted the picture of the future in way that evokes emotion and inspires movement, go back and start over. If you don't, you'll continue to feel you're going in circles, accomplishing nothing, or that all of your efforts are an uphill battle.

A powerful example of bringing vision to life is Martin Luther King Jr.'s "I Have a Dream" speech. I've read the speech hundreds of times, and every time I read it, I get emotionally inspired to make the world a better place. Martin Luther King Jr. was a functional leader who knew how to a paint a vivid picture of the future. He knew how to put humanity at the core of purpose. He ignited forward momentum during a time when the nation desperately needed change. Martin Luther King Jr. shows business leaders throughout the world how to paint a vision of great.

Question 4: How is the business going to achieve the image you just painted?

Only after you paint a vivid picture of the future can you share with people the map for how to get there. And when you give everyone the map, you need to make sure it's not written in Latin! This brings us back to keeping the message simple. "Corporate speak" doesn't work when you're trying to accelerate a business forward and evoke positive emotion. In fact, "corporate speak" becomes one of the greatest roadblocks preventing your business from getting to its destination.

Remember the example from the beginning of the chapter? The new Innovation Building, meeting Bob, and you becoming frantic because you can't find the directions to get to the new building? In business, that's exactly how people feel when they can't understand the language you're using—no matter how important it sounds. The roadmap you provide to your destination has to be in a language everyone understands. If they can't understand the language, they'll never get to the treasure!

Here's an example of the "corporate speak" businesses love to use, and how to translate it into everyday language people actually understand. When you communicate how the business is going to achieve its vision, you need to use language similar to the translations I provide in the following chart. If you can't find the humor, or find yourself grasping onto "corporate speak" with an iron fist, you need to go back to Chapter 1.

Corporate Speak	Translation
Foundational Excellence	The business is going to make sure everyone has the supplies and support to do their job and keep customers happy.
Cultural Efficiencies	The business will start listening to people and use their ideas to create a healthier workplace.
Communicative Leadership	Leaders are to going to talk to people, and make face-to-face conversation a priority.
Operational Effectiveness	The business is going to make sure it doesn't have multiple people doing the same job and that processes aren't redundant.

When you're trying to describe how the business is going to achieve the image you painted, contrary to what you might think, it's not time to get into details. You simply need to identify the top three high-level initiatives that will get the business to its destination—the vivid picture you painted. When it comes to high-level initiatives, choose no more than three. You're looking for the three dominos that will have the highest impact on the rest of the business. If you have more than three, you have too many! It doesn't matter how large your business is, or how much money your business has, four initiatives are too many. Regardless of how smart your initiatives sound, having more than three will double or triple the time it takes your business to get anywhere you want it to go. If you have more than three, you may not even make it to your destination.

In our world of downsizing, acquisitions, and layoffs, you're trying to do more with fewer people. If you have more than three high-level initiatives, you're creating significant energy clogs in the third chakra of your business. People will become increasingly more exhausted and unproductive. Here's the deal: If you hit all three initiatives out of the ballpark and get to your destination sooner than you thought, fantastic! Everyone in the business will be thrilled and energized, and profits will soar. Now you can add three more initiatives to your list!

This often throws leaders off, and I get an immediate, "We need a strategy! We need specific details. You said that we need to give everyone directions!" Yes, you need a strategy and details, and you need to make sure everyone has clear direction. However, functional leaders don't just create a detailed strategy and give it to people. That approach creates robots, fear of failing, and an unhealthy dependency on dysfunctional leaders. Functional leaders provide a high-level view of the top priorities that, when attained, will get the business to realize the vision. After figuring out the top three priorities, functional leaders give the freedom to everyone else in the business to figure out the specific details of how the initiatives are going to happen. Yes, functional leaders still provide support and helpful accountability. However, after the handoff, functional leaders step out of the way and let the smart people they hired do their jobs. That's the next stage of the Destination Map: What's everyone's role?

Question 5: What's everyone's role?

Here's what you've been waiting for—directions! Before you get too excited and create some kind of crazy Gantt chart, remember that *your* role is to give people clear guidance and freedom. When you get to this point in the process, you need to hold back and stop yourself from giving a prescriptive strategy for getting to the destination. If you get prescriptive, you're going to clog the energy system, and all this vision work you've done will get you nowhere. You need to ask everyone in the business one question, and everyone needs to answer it individually. From the part-time janitor to the CEO, everyone needs to answer the question in order to create enough healthy energy to move the business forward. The question is simple: *What is your role in moving the initiatives forward?*

The beauty in the destination process is that the vision is achieved and the business moves forward by giving people—regardless of level, status, or title—the freedom to make the vision their own. The only way anyone will ever make the vision their own is if you make them part of the process. Remember Kerry, the Partner in the large accounting firm in Chapter 1? Kerry was the functional leader who brought her team together and said, "If this company is going to have any hope of attaining our estimated growth rates, let alone not having to lay people off in the next three years, all of you need to be part of building the plan for how we're going to move forward. I don't have all the answers. I'm only one person, with only one mind—that's not going to get us very far. It's going to take all of us. You all have the permission and protection to be as innovative and creative as possible in developing the solutions that will get our projected results." Kerry followed the destination process and it took her business straight to the top by giving people the freedom to use their own brilliance to contribute to and create something great.

To accomplish this stage of the process successfully, you need to own the role of mentor, coach, and accountability partner. People have to become your priority. You have to face the right way—away from the "higher ups" (whatever that means in your world)—and put your efforts toward helping people be the best they can be in their roles. Going back to the driving example at the beginning of the chapter, your role is to make sure everyone gets to the meeting on time so they can make a great first impression with Bob. If people want to create their own Gantt chart to keep things on track—great! Your job is simply to make sure they have all the resources, unwavering support, and accountability they need to succeed along the way.

How One Business Accomplished the Process

Alex is the executive vice president of a large textile business. Three years ago the business leaders realized they had a problem on their hands. After a fairly significant merger with an industry partner, the business started to show an alarming decline in a number of areas. Although revenue was actually better than ever and profits seemed to be holding strong, engagement scores were now sitting at the 75th percentile, attrition spiked to almost 17 percent in some areas of the business, and exit interviews reported that people were leaving because they were exhausted, thought the business lacked direction, and felt that leaders had become callous. Recruiting and retaining new people become increasingly difficult. And the lack of trust that was building would make any future change initiatives virtually impossible. The business was already feeling the pressure, and the pressure started to create leaders who reverted back to an autocratic management style due to being completely exhausted—after working 14-hour days, it was just easier that way. Alex, being a functional leader, could see that regardless of how much money the business was now making, if things didn't seriously change, if the business didn't start taking care of its people, the revenue wave would only last so long before the business found itself crashing without the people who were critical to its future.

Alex and a few other colleagues saw the danger ahead. They knew that the only way to get the business moving back in the right direction was to refuel the business with healthy energy. They knew they had to figure out and communicate a crystal-clear destination and a meaningful purpose, and refocus everyone working for the business on three core initiatives. So that's what they did. They brought together a large group of people comprising all levels and business functions. They hired an outside consultant to facilitate the group through the destination process. And at the end of the session, the group put together a plan that would allow all 90,000 people who were now part of the textile business to own the vision as their own, and together move the business forward in the right direction—toward a work environment that would thrive on healthy energy, and profits that people could feel good about driving. Their plan was simple: *Share. Ask. Document. Support.* And it all happened brilliantly.

Every division leader created a YouTube video that creatively conveyed the vision, purpose, and top three core initiatives. In the video they owned up to the challenges the business had been facing, and they gave a personal commitment to supporting everyone in their own unique role to help move the business forward. In the video the leaders addressed the previous management style, and they gave their word that they would continue to work on their own leadership as well as support all leaders in the business to do the same. The videos were catchy, made people laugh, and, most importantly, each message was authentic and unscripted. The executive leaders, whom most people never even had an opportunity to meet, became real people whom they could trust. The videos were so good that they became viral inside the business, and people began sharing their leader's video with other teams. It was a hit.

At the end of each video, each leader asked for a commitment from everyone to make the vision their own, to creatively develop ways to get to the destination as a team and individually. The message was clear: To move the business forward, it would take everyone, and everyone was given the freedom to add value and contribute to figuring out how it was going to happen. Each video concluded with one question: "What is your role?"

Each leader was asked to have a one-on-one conversation with everyone on his or her specific team. During the conversation, leaders shared their version of the story along with what they believed was their role—to be a mentor, a coach, and an accountability partner. They gave examples of what their role looks like in the day-to-day operation. Then leaders asked the question, *What is your role?*

Understanding that people needed time to think about their role and newfound freedom, the business set up an online portal where each team had a private discussion board. Throughout a 30-day time period, people were asked to share their responses to the question, *What is your role?* And they were asked to describe what they believed a vision of *great* looks like. Within the discussion board, people were able to list specifically what they were going to do to live out their role and help move the company forward. Team members were able to provide feedback, make suggestions, and support one another. Ground rules were set up front, and they were easy: *Support each other, be respectful, and stay within the realm of the three core initiatives.* The portal was a clever way to get people involved, and to document all of the great ideas and specific action plans.

Leaders actually became mentors, coaches, and accountability partners. They met with each person at least every two weeks, even if the conversation had to be over the phone. Each discussion was filled with support and encouragement as they helped people formulate their action plans more thoroughly, celebrate successes, and come up with new ideas. During this time, leaders were able to check in, make sure the destination was still clear, and that people continued to feel good about where the business was going and could continue to articulate how they specifically fit into the big picture. The biggest win? Leaders kept their word. Most leaders never missed a meeting with the people on their team because they made their people the number-one priority. And the people responded tenfold.

Although the business wasn't perfect—no business is—every leader, from the C-suite to front-line supervisors, made the effort to stay true to the Destination Map. The results created an unwavering belief in the process. Engagement reached the 88th percentile by the second year, and the 91st percentile by year three. Attrition averaged 5 percent across the business. Revenue stayed high and steady, while profits increased by 7 percent. Alex and team are still on the road to the ultimate destination, but life in the world of healthy energy feels pretty damn good.

A final word of wisdom about vision and purpose: Be patient. Your business isn't going to reach its destination overnight. In our technologically connected, plugged-in world with information constantly at our fingertips we expect immediate results. Instant gratification is our greatest desire. It's like a drug. We want everything *right now*, and if we don't get it, we move on to the next shiny object. If we would have just waited one second longer, the destination would have been right in front of us. Instead, we decide that one second is too long so we create something new to go after, and all we've created are hundreds, if not thousands, of missed opportunities. We've all heard the old adage, *Good things come to those who wait.* Be patient. Keep your eye on the target. Healthy energy is not going to happen overnight, nor is the business going to arrive at its destination the moment you figure out where it's going. Here's the guarantee: If you apply everything you learned in this chapter, and add patience to the formula, you *will* arrive at the destination faster than you think. When you get there, people will have more energy, and the business will have more money in the bank.

Chapter Highlights

✳ **Vision and purpose ignite forward momentum.**

✳ Principle #2 sits within the third eye chakra of your business. The third eye chakra gives people guidance and wisdom to move forward, and it creates the clear thinking and focus necessary to attain goals and aspirations.

✳ Businesses need both a vision and a purpose. You can't have one without the other. Both are necessary to create an energy ecosystem that drives profits.

✳ If you don't have *functional leaders* delivering the message, your business *will* go back to square one—energetically slimed and going nowhere fast.

✳ Destination Mapping allows people to personally own the vision.

✳ When creating a vision, make it about more than money, make it sustainable, make it impact people and the world, make it bold yet attainable, and keep it simple.

✳ Visually describing the vision in a way that evokes emotion is the key to inspiring people to move the business forward.

✳ Stay away from "corporate speak" as you are sharing with people where the business is going and how it's going to get there.

✳ During the final stage of creating a Destination Map, you need to give people the freedom to create their own unique strategy for getting the business to its destination.

Principle #3
Truth and Clarity Motivate Action

Communication is the delicate balance of silence and words for the benefit of motivation, and it lives within the throat chakra of your businesses. It's within this energy center that the business needs to convey responsibility and decisions with clarity and truth. Similar to a personal relationship, the only way you can have a healthy business that fuels healthy energy is if you, first and foremost have a foundation of truth and clarity. There is no other way. If you take truth and clarity out of the business, you might as well vacuum every ounce of healthy energy out of the people involved in it.

Think about the last bad relationship you were in. Maybe you're in one right now. You know the kind: It starts out great—the honeymoon stage. Staring into each other's eyes, flowers, constant talking, and sharing the world with each other. She's so great or he's so amazing. You find yourself saying, "I think this is it." There's an excitement that speaks of new beginnings. Both of you love everything about each other. Everything you would normally find annoying turns to complete adoration. You're in love. You can't keep your hands off each other. The sex is great and happens all the time. Constant "PDA" and "TMI" annoy the hell out of your friends. Yes, this is the real thing.

Then you start finding out some things that make you go, "Hmmm." For one, he told you he was an owner of a business. It turns out he only works for the business as a sales rep. When you ask him why he told you he owned the business, he simply says, "I am the owner of the business—my part of the business. Good sales reps manage their portion of the business like it's their own. That makes me an owner." You're thinking, *No, that makes you a liar*. Then there was that little weekend trip he took with friends. You accidently found a picture that showed him getting a little too close with one of his friends. When you ask him about the picture, his response is, "We're just friends. I had a little too much to drink. It's no big deal." You say, "Like hell it's not. I thought we were exclusive." He says, "We never *actually* had the exclusive conversation." So now, even though you should run, you have the exclusive conversation.

Time goes on and you still can't get the image of the picture you saw out of your mind. You're obsessed. You start asking all of your friends about it. "Should I leave, should I stay, should I leave, should I stay?" Your friends are yelling, "Run, Forrest, run!" You stay. Bad decision.

More time goes by and everything seems to be going great. You've seen no more incriminating pictures, and you've justified the little lie about being a business owner. Your partner, on the other hand, is becoming increasingly annoyed with the fact that you don't turn off the lights when you leave a room, you leave the water running when you brush your teeth, you don't throw out the carton when you take the last soda, and you don't, well, *think* the way he does. If you did, life would be perfect. You're annoyed with the fact that he seems to pick on you all the time—nag, nag, nag.

It now feels as though you've been together longer than you actually have. The lies are still festering in your head. You begin to question everything he says, because you're not quite sure if he's ever telling you the whole story; you've discovered a few more "nuances" to what he's told you. He has become increasingly annoyed with the fact that you're not acting exactly the way he wants you to, and you're still annoyed with his constant nagging, the exaggerated truths, and the arguments. When you call out his exaggerations you're met with, "I just didn't want to make you mad, rock the boat. You've been working so hard, I didn't want to distract you with the little details that didn't really pertain to you anyway." You're thinking, *WHAT??* And the sex…well, what sex? Even when you do have sex it's blah because neither of you can let go of the thoughts in your head. Resentment and irritability grow. Your 500 texts per day go down to one or two, simply out of feeling obligated to send a text or respond to one. One thing leads to another, and BAM! The relationship is over. Dead.

You spend another five months trying to shake off the bad residue of green energetic slime that resulted from staying way too long in a seriously bad situation. Now all you can think is, *Thank God I got out when I did. Hasta la vista, baby!*

✳✳✳

You're either laughing or crying at the end of that example. Most people in the world have been in a bad relationship at one point or another. And most people feel as though they're in a bad relationship with the business they work for, and they feel stuck in the relationship because of money, status, and insecurity. Being part of a business that lacks truth and clarity does the same thing to our energy as a bad relationship: It sucks our good energy dry, fills us with toxic energy, and lessens our confidence and drive.

The relationship in the example came to its death for the same reason many businesses die—deceit, manipulation, and lies, followed by unsaid expectations that fuel frustration, confusion, and doubt. Just as in a personal relationship, if business leaders don't tell the truth and provide clarity to the people working in the business, the business leaders are choosing to end the relationship. Or even worse, the business relationship becomes filled with abuse, negativity, lack of love, and depression. It turns into the type of relationship that causes everyone on the outside to ask, "Why did she stay in the relationship so long? How could she take it? Didn't she know she could have left and actually experienced a good life? I'm glad I'm not her. How sad."

So what is truth, exactly? The word *truth* seems to cause just as much of a debate in business as the word *ethics*. It has as much power as the word *religion*. And it seems to have turned into a choice among some business leaders, who make their decision to tell the truth based on the amount of impact the truth has on the stock market. *If we tell the truth and there's a chance our stock will go up*, "Yes, let's do it." *If we tell the truth and there's a chance our stock will go down*, "Let's *position* the message to make sure it doesn't appear as though we've lied."

Okay, let's take it back to the relationship example. Remember the party in the relationship who said he was an owner of a business, when in actuality the business had only asked him to treat his piece of the business as though it was his own? That person decided not to share the whole story, and therefore decided to lie in an effort to look better in the eyes of the stakeholder (the person he was in a relationship with). Inevitably, the stock went down and the relationship ended. This personal relationship is no different from a business that makes telling the truth contingent on the stock market.

Truth only exists when the whole story is revealed. In a relationship, if you choose to not provide the whole story, regardless of the situation, you can sit back and watch hurt, resentment, and anger brew within each person while the relationship falls apart around them. A business is no different. If leaders choose to tell the truth based how much money the company will or will not make, and if leaders choose not to disclose the whole story, then everyone in the business can sit back and watch hurt, resentment, and anger brew while the business falls apart around them. Enron is just one example of that reality. If the business is withholding information, it's not providing the whole story. *Truth*, in its pure definition, is the whole story. If business leaders are *purposefully* not providing the whole story, well then, the business is being downright deceitful and manipulative.

Truth and clarity sit within the throat chakra of your business. In comparing a business to a human body, truth and clarity are the breath of the business that moves through the channel of communication. If the communication channel has an airway blockage of manipulation or confusion, the business becomes suffocating to everyone, and no one has the lung capacity to move the business forward. On the flip side, if the inhale is filled with healthy energy fueled with truth and clarity, there's nothing your business can't accomplish—every part of your business becomes filled with vitality.

When a business chooses not to disclose the whole story, it's choosing to block the energy channel of communication—the channel that fuels and purifies the whole energy ecosystem of your business. The channel of communication is life-giving, and goes far beyond the department or position your business calls "internal communications."

Communication

To have a business with a healthy energy ecosystem, you have to bring communication to life. This goes beyond the creation of memos, beyond the tangible items we love to create. I'm talking about the words people choose to speak and write, how the energy behind the true intent of messages impacts others, and how personal energy shows up in your business. Communication fuels movement toward your business destination, and, if toxic, it's powerful enough to take your business down.

Good communication that fuels healthy energy and replenishes a business is threaded with complete truth and clarity. A business suffering from bad communication, vocal or written, can be compared to a smoker suffering from lung cancer—she can't breathe, and every part of her body shuts down. In fact, we can run a lot of parallels between an addicted smoker and business when it comes to communication: With every inhale a smoker takes, she knows that the smoke going into her lungs is horrible for her health. She knows that with every inhale her body's ability to fight off disease lessens. She also knows that the secondhand smoke she's choosing to exhale and give to everyone else is putting other lives in danger. You'd be hard-pressed to find a smoker who doesn't know the research, but many smokers choose to live in denial. That denial kills both themselves and those around them. They keep puffing, their lungs keep coughing, and everyone around them gets to suffer the consequence—lung cancer, emphysema, asthma, and a number of other chronic diseases associated with cigarette smoke. The same thing happens to your business. You see, the smoke from a cigarette is no different from toxic energy that fills a business due to a lack of clarity, vague messages, deceit, manipulation, denial, excuses, and positions that are borderline unethical. You may be thinking, "My business isn't any of these things. We have great communication." Do you, or is that denial talking?

Communication is the throat chakra and breath of your business, so it's the part of your energy ecosystem that needs to be front and center, top of mind, for every leader within your business—period. What do you have to do in order to circulate healthy energy through your business and create a haven of productivity? When it comes to communication that fuels healthy energy, your business has to:

* Lead with positive intent.

* Show up without anger.

* Be transparent.

* Communicate courageously.

* Be strong enough to face fear.

Lead With Positive Intent

Intent is the energetic force behind any message. Anytime words enter the world, there's intent. Whether the words are spoken or written, intent always exits. The intent may be to share information, change someone's mind, express emotion, or create action. The words we choose are always created first by intent. Here's where the truth and clarity thing can go seriously wrong. If the intent of any communication is sour, toxic energy vibrations automatically permeate and impact everyone in the business. Seriously, think about it: Have you ever showed up to a business function and been greeted by someone who didn't like you, or thought you were a threat? He marches right up to you and says in a delighted voice, "Hello, so good to see you. How are you?" Meanwhile, the intent behind his words is really saying, "I thought I got rid of you. Why are you here? If it was up to me, you would just go home." The energetic vibe from the intent itself was strong enough to at least send you away from him in a hurry.

Now take that same intent and apply it to a massive change in your business. For example, you just had your internal communications team write a business-wide e-mail that says, "We are excited about the future and all its possibilities. We're excited to have all of you as part of this amazing journey. In the coming weeks, many of you will have the opportunity to participate in moving these upcoming changes forward...." The intent behind the message is, "Let's just put a message out there that keeps people quiet while we figure out who's getting laid off. We had all the leaders sign NDAs, so we should have plenty of time to work things through." Soon, the energetic vibe that came from the intent contaminates the entire business. Leaders have kept their promise and made sure the layoffs were hush-hush, yet everyone in the business is filled with anxiety when they receive the e-mail. Idle gossip has now turned into, "Did you hear that the business is laying off 200 people? I think you're one of them." Now everyone's looking for their next job, and leaders have been forced to lie, spending their time as therapists mitigating emotional disasters by saying, "I haven't heard of any layoffs. You have nothing to worry about. Just keep focusing on your work."

People have gut feelings. These feelings are called intuition. Human intuition is the human body reading the energy of the intention behind any type of communication. Intuition is designed to protect and guide us toward making the right decision—it drives our internal fight-or-flight reaction. Intuition comes from the body reading energy, and reporting messages to the mind. Have you ever been part of a business that fed you positive lip service while it was going through massive change, only to find out later that your intuition was giving you accurate messages about what was really going on? People's minds are smart, the human body is smarter, and emotions and intuition have them both beat.

When people have clarity, they have a reason to trust you and the business. If your intent is to provide false clarity, people will smell the manipulation a mile away, and the business will end up with energetic green slime that takes years to clean. Make sure the communication happening in your business leads with truthful and positive intent. The future of your business depends on it.

Show Up Without Anger

Have you ever seen a leader get upset and slam a door? Or start yelling for no reason at all? When you see it happen, all you can think is, "Was that really necessary?" The answer is always no. Have you ever found yourself raising your voice and hurting someone's feelings because you were angry about something completely unrelated to the person you hurt? The answer is yes. The answer is yes, because it happens to all of us. If you're human, you have experienced those moments when your own emotions came through as anger to someone in front of you who didn't deserve the wrath.

Your thoughts and emotions create the energetic frequencies you put into the world, and they create your reality. The reality you create has the power to harm or delight everyone around you. If you, or anyone in the business, show up like an angry bird during feeding time, that energy creates discomfort, frustration, and hurt for everyone. Remember, we're all energetically connected. Our thoughts and emotions have significant power over others, whether we want them to or not. The emotion of anger multiples tenfold, and it creates unhealthy energy for everyone. Unhealthy anger stalls performance, accelerates reactive emotion, and creates paralyzing fear throughout the business. Do you really want a bunch of angry birds flying around?

We are all prone to anger—both the giving of it and the receiving of it. No one wants to walk around angry all the time, nor do we want to be around anyone else who's angry all the time. Now here's the reality: Our world—that includes you and everyone else—is suffering from the human energy crisis, and when people are energy-depleted, exhausted, and burned out, they lose control of their thoughts and emotions. As a result, people have become irritable and angry at the world. When people are exhausted, they start swimming in self-pity, feel like a failure, and start showing their worst selves to everyone. When exhausted, people become filled with self-sabotaging thoughts and emotions that create even more internal anger. Then we get angry with ourselves for showing our worst. Shame kicks in. So we bury the shame deep inside ourselves, where we keep all the other shameful moments, and the anger cycle continues. This is not about justifying anger; it's about naming the cause.

Anger fuels destructive body language, disbands open communication and trust, and will suck all personality out of a business—say goodbye to healthy energy and a place where people want to work. Anger will turn productive collaboration into false acts of participation, and teamwork into obligation. Anger can be silent and deadly, or loud and degrading. Either way, the negative energy it creates will suffocate your business. Anger, if it does not turn productive, will fuel Machiavellian political techniques throughout all levels of the business and create energetic lung cancer for everyone.

Here's the beauty: We all get angry, and anger can actually be fantastic. When it's under control, anger is often the emotion that leads to great positive change. For example, people can get angry that chemicals are being dumped in the ocean, and then that anger can turn into a powerful conservation act. We can get angry that someone treated us poorly, and that anger can propel us to stand up for our own truth. Anger can be beautiful and powerful when it's acknowledged for what it is—an emotion ignited by fear. Anger is healthy when it becomes the bridge between fear and courage, used to incite forward motion toward a better existence.

The secret to turning anger into positive change is to be mindfully aware—a high-character value. This is not just a leadership communication skill, this is an *everyone* communication skill. Dr. Marshall B. Rosenberg can help with that. He is the founder of The Center for Nonviolent Communication and the creator of a technique called Nonviolent Communication (NVC), a powerful technique used in more than 60 countries for peacefully resolving differences at personal, professional, and political levels. NVC teaches people how to use mindful communication—a direct connection to mindful awareness. More information on NVC can be found at *www.cnvc.org*.

Anger can be healthy, and healthy anger is driven through mindful awareness. If leaders in your business are showing up with anger repeatedly, and not taking responsibility by moving forward with a positive intent, your business needs to leverage the NVC technique, and your leaders need to get functional. If they don't, then your business will continue to circulate toxic energy and you'll have angry birds everywhere.

Be Transparent

From e-mails to texts to the intranet, people are writing and reading 24/7. Writing is a great art and privilege. People rely on the written language for everything. It's how we communicate messages, transfer information, gain alignment, and stay connected. That being said, "You can't believe everything you read" is a statement that holds true in many businesses. To fuel healthy energy, you need to make sure that the messages being written in your business are transparent and free from deceit, manipulation, and lies. If the words you're choosing do not deliver a clean message, the whole story, and a positive intent, people will sense deceit a mile away. When they do, your business throws trust right out the window, and the toxic energy those words create will destroy the productivity of your business. People will go from wanting to work for you, to having to force themselves to show up and do the bare minimum just to get paid. No one wants to do anything for someone who uses deceit to manipulate their actions. You need to ensure that your business is not using the art of writing as a form of manipulation. It happens more than you think, especially when the financial stakes appear high.

Transparency is the bridge between truth and clarity, and it's the action that keeps a business honest. Transparency is how a business delivers the whole story and presents all the details. Transparency is the living action of truth. You might be thinking, *A business can't always be transparent.* Spin it however you want from a business leader's point of view:

* We don't want too much information getting out. If all the information came out it would be detrimental to revenue and profits, and our stock would go down.

* We don't want to rock the boat and harm performance.

* We don't want to take people's focus away from what they really need to be doing.

* They don't need to know all that information to do their job.

* They can't handle the truth!

Here's the deal: The truth is going to come out sooner or later. All the information will reveal itself, whether you want it to or not. If you're not transparent, the truth will start as gossip, and people will take the gossip as truth because that's the only "information" they have to hang onto. A leader may break under pressure and share everything with a line-level friend, and that line-level friend will share her version of the truth with everyone else. Before you know it, the news has spread like wildfire. Now the business has to spend hours fixing, smoothing over, and making excuses for why it wasn't transparent to begin with—not to mention the effort that now has to go into rebuilding trust, rather than nurturing the trust that already exists. Rebuilding is always more costly than maintenance.

As a business leader, you have choice. You can choose to be transparent by delivering truth and clarity with conviction, or you can you choose to only deliver a partial message that causes confusion and emotional turmoil. For every leader there is a defining moment: Someone *will* ask you to withhold the whole story. If you do, the people in your business will see you as a liar. I get it; you're in a high-profile business, and some very important people who make six or seven figures are telling you to "Keep it a secret. Don't show anyone. For your eyes only—and only while you're in the club of leadership." I get your reality, but here's the deal: If you choose to continue the dysfunction by not sharing the whole story, you are a liar. That personal label never feels good, and it's incredibly difficult to get rid of.

Let's take it a step further. If you're not being transparent, you can't justify being frustrated that people aren't doing what the business needs them to do. Going back to Chapter 2, it's like giving someone the vision without the directions on how to get there, and then getting upset because they show up late. When someone has clarity because he inherently knows that he's being told the whole story, he's motivated to move the business forward.

When was the last time you were excited, motivated, and inspired to do something nice for someone who was deceitful and manipulative to you? When was the last time you walked up to your significant other or friend and said, "I really wish you were a complete liar. That's the type of person I want to be around. That's the type of person I want to give my all to. That's the type of person who gives me energy." Yeah, the green kind that comes in the form of slime. Yuck! If you think this is harsh, you're right; it is. And it needs to be, because it's the truth. It's the whole story that no one wants to talk about. Or it's talked about, but we don't allow it to get personal. We justify it by saying "It's my job." No, it's not. It's called leadership dysfunction at its best.

We convenience ourselves that being a liar is okay as long as we're getting paid to do it. The more we get paid, the more we're asked to lie. The more we lie, the more toxic energy gets dumped into the business. You and everyone one else in the business are now caught in a cycle of perpetual deceit that generates enough destructive energy that your whole body feels like it's stuck in cement and you can't move anywhere—certainly not forward. Yet we still go back to justifying it. Hell, we even feel important when we make it to the top and get to be one of the few people who not only know the whole story but also get to lie about it. When you look at it from the perspective of being in a personal relationship, you know it's sick, demented, and wrong.

Just thinking about being on the other side of deception is enough to give anyone anxiety and heartache. Think about the last time you were lied to, the last time you were impacted by someone who chose not be transparent and give you the whole story. Do you remember the feeling of heaviness? Can you feel it now just thinking about it? That heaviness you're feeling is the toxic energy that lives in a business when the business is unhealthy. It's the same heaviness that every person, from the part-time janitor to the CEO, gets to carry when the business chooses to withhold truth. It's the heaviness that businesses are asking leaders at all levels to deliver to the rest of the people in the business. Congratulations—you've made it to the top. Now the question is, do you have the courage to change it?

Communicate Courageously

Courage is moving toward something, no matter how scary or unknown, in order to make your life better, your business more successful, and the world a better place to live. If you want to energize people, ignite action, and drive profits in the future, you have to have courage, and you have to exercise courageous communication. Courageous communication is about standing up for what you believe is right, and stepping forward to change what may be perceived as normal, but what you know in your heart is wrong. It's about putting truth and clarity first and being unwilling to communicate, through speech or writing, anything that doesn't align with the whole story. It's about giving up control and trusting the brilliant minds of the people who work for the business with the whole truth and nothing but the truth.

As we've learned, the people in your business are exhausted, and a large part of their exhaustion stems from their constant search for truth. They wait for any opportunity to read new communication, have a conversation with a leader, or go to an all-staff meeting in hopes that they will finally learn what's going on with the business, how they will be impacted, and the role they get to play in helping the business move forward. People are tired of games, and they don't want to fight for the right information anymore. If they have to keep fighting for information and clarity, they will leave your business and go work somewhere else. That's not cutting fat, that's losing your best talent—because your best talent *will* leave first.

The business leaders who have the courage to communicate with truth and transparency will be the leaders who win the future. The leaders who have the courage to stand up to the C-suite, their peers, their teams, and their stockholders, and actually speak the whole story with complete truth and clarity, will be the leaders who overcome all challenges in the future. Yes, courage takes vulnerability, and it's high-character leaders who will embrace this vulnerability and move your business forward. These are the leaders you want in your business. These are the leaders who will be instrumental in refueling your greatest business asset: human energy.

When I think of courage I'm reminded of the 1997 Apple ad, "Here's to the Crazy Ones":

> "Here's to the crazy ones. The misfits. The rebels. The troublemakers. The round pegs in the square holes. The ones who see things differently. They're not fond of rules, and they have no respect for the status quo. You can quote them, disagree with them, glorify, or vilify them. But the only thing you can't do is ignore them. Because they change things. They push the human race forward. And while some may see them as the crazy ones, we see genius. Because the people who are crazy enough to think they can change the world, are the ones who do."

Be Strong Enough to Face Fear

We can't talk about courage without talking about fear. Fear is everywhere in business. It breeds dysfunction. If you want healthy communication that energizes people, ignites action, and drives profit in your business, fear is your worst enemy. It's paralyzing.

Fear paralyzes people's ability to do their best work. Fear puts us into a cage surrounded by a life we don't want. Fear forces businesses to spend money that doesn't need to be spent. If you want revenue, profits, energy, and a business that's fueled to win in today's market, you have to hit fear head-on. Reducing fear is the greatest cost reduction your business will ever experience—period. And eliminating harmful fear is the only thing that will unlock the restraints that the business has put on courageous communication—a non-negotiable if you want to increase human energy.

Fear is the reason leadership dysfunction exists. Leaders have a fear of being vulnerable, a fear of taking a risk because they fear consequences. They say things such as:

* I'll lose my golden handcuffs.

* I won't make as much if I go somewhere else.

* I'm too old to change careers now.

* No one else will want me.

That fear prevents them from being high-character leaders. It prevents them from making the positive change your business so desperately needs. It stops them from making courageous decisions to speak and write the truth. If you want people to feel good again and to perform at their best, and you want your business to be fueled by healthy energy, then you have no choice but to get your leaders to face their fears and become functional.

The only way your business will create functional leaders is through the leadership development process given in Chapter 1. The business has to hold leaders accountable by tying the expectation of living high-character values to the money each leader earns—their personal profit center. The business has to make sure each leader is receiving energy work, and the business needs to create a mentor program in which leaders can actually see others who have authority modeling the way of functional behavior. ***Don't skip the energy*** *work.* It's different, it's new, and leaders want to skip it because of fear. If your business is going to take fear on, every leader needs to take a chance by doing something outside their comfort zone. That's what courage is—moving toward something new no matter how scary or unknown it may be, in order to make life better, and your business more successful. Fear is simply fuel for courage. Put it in its place. Be bold. All your business needs to do is name fear out loud and do what it takes to move past it—functionally.

✳✳✳

Remember Sarah from Chapter 1? Sarah was the Director of Communications for a high-profile healthcare company. During two recalls on the company's most profitable over-the-counter drugs, Sarah was instrumental in successfully influencing senior leaders to own up to the fact that the recall was due to errors in the manufacturing plant. She wrote the communication strategy that brilliantly positioned the company to consumers as an ethical brand, and fully disclosed the details of the occurrence to people throughout the business. Because of Sarah's courage and strength to stand strong in what was right, regardless of the repercussions, the business and Sarah became highly respected. Rather than hitting the job boards with disgust, people became inspired and motivated to be working for an organization that was willing to be transparent at all costs in order to protect humanity from a potentially deadly outcome. Sarah faced fear head-on and won.

Communication in your business is not limited to the department or position in your business that creates memos, newsletters, and intranet content. It's not just the people in your business who arrange town hall meetings and leadership events. Communication is the delicate balance of silence and words for the benefit of motivated action. It's the vocal and written words that live within the throat chakra of your business, and it's within this energy center where the business needs to convey responsibility and decisions with clarity and truth.

Communication, and everything it's composed of, is the energetic air purifier for your business. If the filter in your air purifier is dirty, all that energetic slime just keeps getting recirculated into the business like contaminated air on a plane—people keep breathing in the toxic energy and get sick. When the people in your business are energetically sick, they don't perform at their best. Not only does performance go down, but your best employees leave your business to go work somewhere else. The fix is easy: Make sure the communication filters are clean. If the filters are clean, everyone gets to breathe healthy energy, performance goes up, and voilá! You again have more money in the bank.

✷✷✷

Now it's time to start building the throat chakra of your energy ecosystem. Communication sits within the throat chakra, and it's the airway for the breath of your business. The throat chakra of your business becomes healthy and circulates energy when you make sure everyone understands and is able to apply Micro Destination Mapping and Nonviolent Communication.

The Process: Micro Destination Mapping

Micro Destination Mapping is similar to the Destination Mapping Process presented in Chapter 2, but at an individual and small-group level. In an energetically healthy business, Micro Destination Mapping is the communication format for one-on-one conversations, written messages, and/or any presentation, no matter how small. The micro version of the process ensures people are crystal-clear on the intent of the message, and it makes leaders think through how and why they're communicating prior to jumping into delivering the message.

Your business needs to teach everyone this mapping process for two reasons: One, because it's a foundational communication process that ensures that truth and clarity circulate throughout your business, resulting in healthy energy flow. Two, if everyone understands and can identify the process, your business has created an internal accountability system for truth and clarity. Your business also needs to incorporate the skill of Micro Destination Mapping as a measureable performance observation within all review systems, creating a more tangible form of accountability and the expectation that everyone should communicate in a way that fuels healthy energy. The process is used both for vocal and written communication. Here's what the mapping process looks like.

* **Stage 1: State your true intent.** This should be the first sentence out of your mouth or out of your pen. The intent is *why* you're communicating. The intent may be to change minds, provide information, or create action. You need to make sure your intent is positive. If you're not confident that your intent will be seen as positive to the person(s) receiving the message, don't communicate the message. If you do, people will know the intent is sour and you'll contaminate the energy airway of your business.

* **Stage 2: Give people the destination up front.** If the communication is successful, *where* will it get you, the people receiving the message, and the business? Everyone loves to jump to the *how* before making the destination crystal clear—that's like asking someone to get into a car and drive without telling them where they're going. Before you jump into the *how*, you need to clearly state the *where*.

* **Stage 3: Paint a vivid picture of the destination.** Even in a one-on-one conversation, you need to paint a picture of the destination. If you don't, it's no one's fault but your own if the communication accomplishes nothing. A vivid image describes what the destination looks like, feels like, and tastes like. This is how you help people emotionally connect, to the message. When people emotionally connect they want to support you. If you skip this stage, all you have are sterile words and an apathetic message that goes nowhere.

* **Stage 4: Give the roadmap.** Here's where you share how the destination you just vividly painted will be reached. Remember losing your directions while driving to the Innovation Building to meet Bob? If you want to reach the destination, you need to be crystal clear on *how* you believe the destination will be reached.

* **Stage 5: Ask for input.** Ask for input, and be willing to in-corporate the feedback—there may be a hundred different ways to get to where you want to go. If you are unwilling to ask and receive input don't communicate the message at all. Energetically healthy businesses thrive on reciprocity. Energy itself is a form of constant reciprocity. Energetically healthy businesses understand that everyone's feedback, regardless of the person's level within the business, is important and should be taken seriously if the business wants to move for-ward successfully.

* **Stage 6: Ask for commitment.** No matter how small the communication, everyone giving or receiving the message has a role and needs to make a commitment—but they're not go-ing to make it, and follow through, unless you ask for it. The commitment might be as easy as agreeing to read the infor-mation, complete a series of tasks, or be a sponsor and influ-ence change from the top. Regardless of the commitment, if you don't ask for it you'll never get what you want.

* **Stage 7: Do your part and follow up.** You need to follow up with everyone who received the communication, gave you input, or made a commitment. If someone gave you input, you need to let her know how you incorporated it, or provide specific reasons why the input was unable to be used—the reasons need to be valid and make sense to everyone involved. If the intent of the communication was to create action, then the follow-up needs to clearly state the progress. And if a commitment was made, send an e-mail to everyone involved

that summarizes the agreement. Most importantly, let people know how much you appreciate their input and effort toward the destination.

The Process: Nonviolent Communication (NVC)

Your business needs to teach everyone, not just leaders, Nonviolent Communication, a powerful technique used in more 60 countries for peacefully resolving differences at personal, professional, and political levels. It is based on four foundational steps, but extends far beyond those steps with practice. Although it may appear so in a quick read, NVC is *not* a robotic "say and do" communication process. The intent is that the steps become a natural occurrence in everyday communication—personally and professionally. NVC is a practice of mindful awareness, a high-character value exhibited by functional leaders. The following is a snapshot of the foundational steps.

✳ **Step 1: Make an objective observation.** Stemming from the value of mindful awareness, Step 1 in the NVC process is about having the ability to objectively look at a situation in the heat of the moment before making a decision on how to react. The technique teaches you how to name the situation without subjective judgment getting in the way. An example is, rather than saying, "It's hot outside," you say, "It's 75 degrees outside." You can't argue the fact that it really is 75 degrees, but you can debate all day about the difference between hot and cold. When people in business are unable to be mindfully aware, they make statements that are often perceived as judgments—such as the idea that 75 degrees is hot. Judgments can cause conflicts, unnecessary debates, and unhealthy emotional responses.

* **Step 2: Name the emotion.** Emotions can get in the way and out of control when we try to run from them or pretend they don't exist. People are great at running from emotion, especially when their emotions ask them to face fear. It's only after you name your emotion that you can figure out what you really want—that want in NVC is called your need.

* **Step 3: State the need.** It's all about needs in business and in life—what "I" need, what "they" need. One of the reasons we're all so tired is that we're not getting our needs met. After you figure out how to name your emotion, coming up with the associated need is easy. Core needs may include wellbeing, connection with other people, and the ability to express what's on our mind. When you're able to state your emotion alongside your need, people are much more willing to help you get your need met.

* **Step 4: Make a request.** Not a demand, directive, or assignment. It's a request to get your need. Be polite when making your request, no matter how high up you are in the business or how entry-level the person you're talking to may be. Everyone in the business needs to be treated as exactly what they are—a human being with a brain who deserves respect. Additionally, contrary to what some might think, regardless of role, people are allowed to say no to your request, and they have the right to make a request of you. That's the fantastic part of the process. NVC fuels a true conversation that gets to the root of people, evens the playing field of respect, and in doing so fuels healthy energy because everyone feels valued.

Sounds simple enough, right? But it's not so easy when you're in the throes of anger or experiencing heavy emotion and exhaustion. This is why it's important that everyone in the business learn NVC. This technique is a requirement if you have any aspirations toward creating a successful energy ecosystem for your business. Without everyone in your business understanding and using NVC, your business increases its chances of building an energy ecosystem that will fail. A book that can help you and your team begin using NVC is *What We Say Matters: Practicing Nonviolent Communication*, by Judith Hanson Lasater and Ike K. Lasater. It's a great first entry into learning how to apply Nonviolent Communication.

Chapter Highlights

✳ **Truth and clarity motivate action.**

✳ Internal communication lives within the throat chakra of your businesses, and it's within this energy center that the business needs to convey responsibility and decisions with clarity and truth.

✳ When people receive the truth, and clearly understand the intent and direction of the messages they're being given, they become emotionally connected and motivated to act.

✳ Most people feel as though they're in a bad relationship with the business they work for. And they feel stuck in the relationship because of money, status, and insecurity.

✳ The channel of communication in your business is life-giving and goes far beyond the department or position your business calls "internal communications."

✳ When it comes to internal communications that fuel healthy energy, your business has to lead with positive intent, show up without anger, be transparent, have courage, and be strong enough to face fear.

✳ If leaders choose to tell the truth based how much money the company will or will not make, and choose not to disclose the whole story, then everyone in the business can watch hurt, resentment, and anger brew while the business falls apart around them.

✳ The third chakra of your business becomes healthy and circulates energy when you make sure everyone understands, and is able to apply, Micro Destination Mapping and Nonviolent Communication techniques.

Principle #4

People Are Driven to Live Out a Purpose

Do you wake up every morning searching for something? Something that seems to be intentionally hiding from you, like you're playing hide and seek with a 5-year-old? You're a competent adult, but the 5-year-old keeps beating you, and the search is becoming exhausting. You're getting frustrated because you know this *thing* is somewhere but you can't figure out where it is. In fact, you're even questioning what it is you're looking for. Yet, you know that if you search long and hard enough, you'll find it. You know you can't stop searching. In fact, you don't want to stop searching. It's almost an obsession that you can't name, but you know that the moment you find this thing you're looking for you'll finally feel good again. You'll be able to breathe. Enjoy life. Damn, where is it?

The search I'm talking about is the search for your purpose—your life purpose. You might be thinking, *Why are you talking about this in a business book? I bought a business book, not a self-help book.* Here's the reality: You can't separate your business life from your personal life. You can try, but it's not possible. Our energy is our energy. It doesn't matter if you're at home, at work, in the car, with your kids, or with your dog, your energy and who you are remain exactly the same. When people are on a constant search for their purpose, they become absolutely exhausted, easily frustrated with life, and the energy they put into the word is that of frustration, exhaustion, and irritation. Home or work, it makes no difference where you are; if you're on the search for your purpose, everything you do is impacted by the exhaustion you carry with you.

The idea of searching for one's purpose often gets confused with searching for something tangible. People say things like, "I'm looking for *it*. I can't find *it*. What is *it*?" Here's the deal: It's not an *it*. Purpose is not a noun. Purpose is a verb. Your purpose shows up in how you show up to live your life. It's not a *thing* that's waiting to be found. Anthony discovered this truth when his life took a surprising turn.

Anthony is the director of business development of a mid-sized manufacturing company. He always tells people the company just makes widgets and whatnots for automobiles—nothing special, just the parts that hold the engine together. Anthony's job is to figure out new ways to grow the business, gain new strategic partners, and make sure that the internal communications, marketing, and sales teams are all playing nice together. Anthony has been with the company for seven years, and has always seemed to enjoy what he does. His comments to friends usually sound like, "I don't do anything too special. I just keep the operation going, and I'm good at it."

When Anthony was 5 years old, he had fire truck. It was a wooden fire truck with a yellowish-orange ladder given to him by his great uncle. Anthony can remember playing with it for endless hours, loving every minute. He made truck noises, ran it into "challenges," and saved endless numbers of cats out of trees. He felt amazingly free anytime he had the opportunity to play with his truck—which was every day, as far as he can remember. Anthony even slept with the fire truck. He loved this truck more than anything.

Fast-forward 40 years. Anthony works, on average, 12 hours a day at the manufacturing business. He's in a decent relationship with a woman he's been with for years. He spends his time going to sports games and hanging out with friends. Each day seems to be the same normal stuff—work, relationship, and outings with friends if there's time left over. Most of his energy goes into his work. Again, he likes it. He's always been good at it, and he likes the feeling of being "successful." However, in the past couple of years, he's started to feel different. It started with an increase in stress at work. His business added five new products to its portfolio, which doubled his effort and added hours onto his workday. The basic ups and downs of his relationship started to challenge his ideas of the future. Free time with friends started to be a minimal luxury. Anthony, normally a guy who genuinely likes life, started to become irritable, frustrated, and absolutely exhausted.

Now, instead of waking up and going about his day satisfied with the status quo, he wakes up finding himself questioning why he continues to subject himself to what seems to be an endless path of workday hours. He wakes up questioning his relationship and what he wants from life. He's been feeling unsatisfied, and almost uncomfortable in his own skin. He often thinks, *What the hell is going on? Why am I feeling this way? I just want to feel good again.* The ups and downs continue, and he finds himself feeling increasingly more unhappy with his life, but he doesn't exactly know why, or how to go about changing things. Time goes on and Anthony keeps questioning, but not changing anything. Even though many things in his life no longer feel as though they fit, he keeps going. Soon, everything in his life is impacted by how he feels on the inside—negative and stuck.

A few months ago he randomly started to think about his fire truck—having no idea why. He would find himself driving to work and then all of a sudden he would have a memory of crashing his fire truck into a tree or the leg of the couch. He could hear his 5-year-old self say, "Crash!" The thought of it was enough to put a huge smile on his face that stayed there all the way to the office. When he got there, he would shake his head as though he had to erase the thought from his mind lest someone find out he was thinking about his fire truck. At times he would even find himself feeling guilty for thinking about something that made him feel so good.

Anthony continued to work through his days, trying his best to avoid the random thoughts that almost seemed to be a glimpse of a more satisfying life. He continued to make excuses to himself in an effort to dodge the reality that he was miserable, and that every ounce of his being was screaming at him to change. The thoughts and emotions didn't go away. Thoughts of what life could be kept surfacing, and it became increasingly more difficult for him to find joy in the everyday life he was living. Work became more difficult, his personal relationships became more trying, and it felt as though someone was sucking his energy dry. He was turning into someone he didn't like, and was almost unrecognizable to himself at times.

One day, out of the blue, as though someone had hit him over the head with his fire truck, he woke up. Without even realizing what was happening, words came out of his mouth: "I don't want to live a life full of obligation and expectation that I don't even want. I want to actually enjoy waking up and going to work again. I want to live life the way I want to live it, not the way everyone else in this world is telling me to live. I want to enjoy everything in life as much I enjoyed that damn fire truck." That was the day Anthony changed. That was the day he started to enjoy life again. He stopped trying to live for everyone else, and he started to live for himself. He took back control of his life, and made healthy changes that helped him feel good again. Anthony ditched the things that were holding him back, and he added some things that he always wanted. Through the process he found the elusive "it." He found his fire truck—a life full of purpose. He was motivated to *live* life again, and everything, including the business he worked for, benefited.

Anthony is no different from the people you have working in your business; many of them are miserable because they're living life in a way that doesn't align with who they really want to be. Everyone in your business wants to find their fire truck—a life full of purpose and meaning. When they do, there's nothing they can't accomplish. Now more than ever people are searching for their purpose, desperately trying to find ways to feel good again. People in your business *will* have that moment when they wake up and find themselves saying, "I don't want to live a life full of obligation and expectation that isn't true to how I want to live. I want to actually enjoy waking up and going to work again." If your business isn't set up to help people spread their wings and fly, they will leave your business and go work somewhere they can honor their own life purpose.

Your best talent will leave first. They will get to the point where the paycheck doesn't matter—no matter how large. They'll hit a breaking point and just leave. If you want to fuel your business, energize people, and drive profits by increasing the healthy energy flow in your business, then you have to create opportunities for people to *want to* be part of the business—on their own terms, and in their own way. You have to create experiences that make people want to stay because being part of the business makes them feel good. People need to have a genuine belief that the business has their best interests in mind.

The only way you're going to fuel your business with healthy energy is if people genuinely feel that your business is helping them live their purpose. When your business helps people live their purpose, people want to help your business live *its* purpose. You *cannot* have it the other way around if you want an energy ecosystem that works. The purpose of every individual person in your business needs to come first. There is no exception. In fact, you wouldn't want it any other way, because when people show up to your business in a way that allows them to live their purpose your business benefits tenfold. The energy that comes from the people who authentically live their truth is the same energy you need to help move your business to its destination.

I'm not suggesting you throw out all your processes and systems so that everyone can find their fire truck. I'm also not suggesting that you make your business a free-for-all where everyone gets to hang out like they're at Woodstock (although that would be fun). I am suggesting that you take a serious look at your business and assess whether it provides opportunities for people to figure out their purpose, and whether there is flexibility in the operating model that allows people to align what they do for the business with their personal value system. To successfully build a healthy energy ecosystem you must create both opportunity to discover and flexibility to live out the discovery. The process that will help your business provide such opportunity and flexibility is called the Performance Through Purpose Campaign. The campaign is a distinct support system that is designed to refuel your people with healthy energy—energy that will allow people to become more engaged in your business. It's a campaign that gets personal, and encourages people to be human and real, to authentically show up to the business in a way that gives them back healthy energy and puts healthy energy back into the business.

The Process: The Performance Through Purpose Campaign

When your business helps people live their purpose, people want to help your business live its purpose. In effort to accomplish this golden rule of energy-based business, you need to help people figure out their purpose. Then you need to give them an environment where they feel safe to spread their wings and fly.

This process will not work if people don't feel safe and supported by the leaders of the business. If your leaders aren't yet functional, leadership functionality needs to be the first priority. The crown chakra of your business needs to be flowing with healthy energy before the business can even hope to free its thymus chakra from toxic energy.

The Performance Through Purpose Campaign helps everyone in the business identify their true life purpose, and gives people the opportunity to live their purpose in the business. The intent of the process, which runs consistently through one year, is to facilitate people through a series of experiences that allow them to discover and live their purpose. The outcome is that the business begins to thrive on healthy energy, and people become more productive and feel good about the work they're doing. The campaign is based on three core experiences:

1. **The Values Inquiry.**

2. **The Credo.**

3. **Living "It" Out Loud.**

The Values Inquiry

The first phase of the campaign is called the Values Inquiry, and it's a one-month process. The intent of the experience is for everyone in the business to be able to identify their personal values, articulate why their values are important, and discover how their values show up in their life. The outcome is that people in the business begin seeing and acknowledging themselves as unique individuals who are both worthy of healthy energy and deserving of the opportunity to live life in a way that honors who they are personally. Value Inquiry is the campaign springboard, and will set the stage for all proceeding campaign efforts.

Values are how we name what we find important and what gives us energy. Like the flour and eggs that help a cake become a cake, values are the ingredients that make up our purpose. You need to ask every person in the company, "What are *your* values?" Not the values of the business, or the values of a certain leader. This is the foundational step toward people figuring out their purpose in life. Remember, you, as the business, are not asking the question for the benefit of the business. You are simply creating an opportunity for self-discovery.

Before people state their values, ask them the following reflective questions. Once they answer the questions, have them identify what values show up in their response. People will typically be able to come up with at least three core values after answering each question. In order for people to answer the question, you'll need to guide them through the process and provide them with personal support throughout the inquiry. (Later in the chapter you'll read how one business integrated the Value Inquiry process into its internal marketing plan.)

* What moment has been the highlight of your life? Describe it. Why was it a highlight? Who was there? What did the environment look like, feel like, sound like? What words were spoken or written? How did you feel, and why? What value was being respected or honored?

* Describe a moment when you have felt wronged. Who or what wronged you? What did the environment look like, feel like, sound like when it happened? What words were spoken or written? How did you feel, and why? What value was being disrespected or hurt?

Here are examples of values adopted from The Leadership Challenge by Kouzes & Posner, that people can reference as a springboard:

✳ **Ambition:** aspiring, hard-working, striving.

✳ **Broad-mindedness:** open-ended, flexible, receptive.

✳ **Being caring:** appreciative, compassionate, loving, nurturing.

✳ **Competence:** capable, proficient, effective, efficient, professional.

✳ **Cooperativeness:** collaborative, team player, responsive.

✳ **Courageousness:** bold, daring, fearless, gutsy.

✳ **Dependability:** reliable, conscientious, responsible.

✳ **Determinedness:** dedicated, resolute, persistent, purposeful.

✳ **Being family-oriented:** relationships, bonding, love.

✳ **Fair-mindedness:** unprejudiced, objective, forgiving.

✳ **Being forward-looking:** visionary, foresighted, sense of direction.

✳ **Growth:** continuous learning, development, achievement.

✳ **Integrity:** truthful, honest, trustworthy, has character.

✳ **Imaginativeness:** creative, innovative, curious.

✳ **Independence:** self-reliant, self-sufficient, self-confident.

✳ **Being inspirational:** uplifting, enthusiastic, energetic, positive about future.

✳ **Intelligence:** bright, thoughtful, intellectual, reflective, logical.

✳ **Loyalty:** faithful, dutiful, unswerving in allegiance, devoted.

✳ **Maturity:** experienced, wise, has depth.

* **Mentorship:** providing guidance and development for others.

* **Renewal:** being a catalyst for change.

* **Self-control:** restrained, self-disciplined.

* **Straightforwardness:** direct, candid, forthright.

* **Spirituality:** believing and honoring what is greater than yourself.

The intent of the experience is to get to the root of what people find important in life, so they can start doing more of the things that give them energy and put healthy energy into the business. The moments in life that people see as "highlights" are those moments when their values were honored. The opposite is true for the moments when people have felt wronged or hurt. When people reflect on these moments it becomes easier to name the values that are important to them and give them energy. Naming your values answers the question everyone is asking: *What is my purpose?*

The reality is, it's our personal values everyone should be searching for—not our purpose. Purpose is easy. The tough part is having the courage to make choices that align your life with your values. When you do, all of sudden you've magically found your purpose—ahh, there "it" is. To help illustrate this point, I'll share my story, my search for "it." Here's some of how I finally found my fire truck.

When I first did this type of Values Inquiry exercise, I was searching for the big "it." I was sitting in a workshop, when the facilitator presented a values exercise. I thought, *Whatever; this will be an interesting exercise, and then I'm sure we'll move onto the good stuff.* Remember, I was on the quest for "it." I wanted my fire truck by 5 p.m. because I had another event to get to.

The facilitator said, "Take a moment and look over the list of values at your table, and choose the ones that are most important to you." I looked at the list for about five minutes and chose my values. My competitive side was quite proud of the fact that I was done before everyone else because I knew myself so well. Yeah, right.

After we chose our values, the facilitator took us through a serious of questions that started to dig into life experience. After I thoughtfully answered each question, it wasn't long before my eyes got big, my mouth opened, and everyone at the table heard me breathe in loudly with shock. When I stared at the values I initially chose, I realized they weren't mine. But that wasn't the shocking part. The shocking part was that I realized that the values I chose, because I knew myself so well, were actually a combination of the values of my employer, my parents, and certain extended family members. I just sat there and stared at a new sheet of values, unable to fill it out. It was in that moment I realized that I didn't know myself at all. I had been living life to appease everyone and everything around me, except me.

One thing led to another, and in time I was able to figure out my true values. I finally figured out what was important to me, and I found a way to describe what my heart was trying to tell me all along. That was the easy part. Here's where I got freaked out: Once I figured out my values, I also figured out that only 5 percent of my life actually aligned with what was important to me. That's when I said, "Oh, shit." You see, it was in that moment that I knew my life was about to get shaken up.

Let me be clear: This "shake-up" did not happened overnight. In fact, it happened throughout an eight-year time period. Admittedly, not everything was beautifully planned. I didn't always go with the flow. Looking back, I now know that simply being aware and naming what I wanted from life ignited a series of events that got me to where I am today. It's amazing what happens when we put intention into the world.

The following paragraphs showcase my real values. Some people may have the same values but interpret them differently, and that's okay. No one else can tell you the right definition for your values. Defining your values is something only you can do.

Spirituality: Believing and honoring what is greater than myself

The significant wakeup call for me in the area of spirituality was the fact that my spirituality had absolutely nothing to do with religion. This may seem obvious to some, but for me, a person who grew up with a traditional religious background, who always heard what would happen to you if you didn't live a certain practice, this concept ignited a ton of fear. *What would people say? What would my family think? What else can I identify with? What am I, if I am not that?* Scary questions, questions that we all find ourselves asking at some point, for one reason or another. For me, the wakeup call was that the practice of religion was actually getting in the way of me being able to honor my value of spirituality. The practice of religion, for me, created restraints of guilt that held me back and depleted my energy. Just the thought of scheduling time for something that depleted my energy was exhausting. So I gave myself permission to not be held back anymore. I gave myself permission to no longer go through the motions of a being part of a belief system that didn't align with who I am. I *owned* the fact that I felt more fulfilled and more spiritually centered, and could give more to this world, when I spent time in nature, meditation, and walking and sitting in the sun on a beautiful day, rather than falsely practicing a belief system to appease others. I got more energy when I allowed myself to see everyone in this world as one. I became more free with acts of generosity, kindness toward others, and understanding in the face of adversity when I took the time to breathe in acoustic music, and sip my coffee on a weekend morning while connecting to and honoring what is greater than myself. I gave myself permission to ditch the guilt, ditch the worry about other people's perceptions, and ditch societal restraints. I figured out what my value of spiritualty meant for me, and I changed what I was doing in my life that no longer aligned with who I am. That was a moment when I started to reclaim my energy. That was a moment that got me closer to naming my purpose in this world.

Truth: Authentically showing up to life, being transparent, and always revealing the whole story

This was a value of mine that showed up in a way that I least expected. The value was easy to name. I thought, *Of course I value transparency, knowing the whole story, and authentically showing up to life. It's just how I live my life. This one's going to be easy.* The reality was that this was the last of my values I figured out how to live.

I was in an energy session one day, getting work done by a new practitioner. I thought, *This will be fun. I'll let someone new practice on me for free. She'll go through the motions and I'll get to relax. Why not?* She did a lovely job reading her manual, going through the steps, and making sure she was doing everything "right"—and then it happened. She says to me, "You have a block in your sacral chakra." I'm thinking, *Yeah, it's the energy center where everything about relationships exists. Not surprising that I have an energy block, but I thought I took care of all those issues.* She keeps talking: "It has to do with forgiveness." I'm thinking, *Again, thought I took care of those issues. I should be flowing freely. Not sure what's going on here.* Then she asks me, "Have you forgiven yourself?" I just look at her and think, *Damn it.*

After I went through my "FINE, whatever" moment, I took a deep breath and answered the question, "I guess not. I suppose that might be a good thing to do. Yep. So what am I forgiving myself for again?" She just looked at me with no expression and said, "I think everything." At that point I really didn't have anything else to say except, "Oh. Okay. That actually makes complete sense. I'll work on that. Thanks." And then she moved on.

She moved on, and I cried. Like a baby. Many moments of just bawling followed that experience with the new energy practitioner. Here's the outcome: I realized that I wasn't living my value of truth because I wasn't being truthful to myself. I figured out that the only way I could be truthful to myself is if I forgave myself for every moment I showed up in this world with imperfections. Because until I forgave myself, I ran from myself. When I ran from myself, avoiding the thoughts about myself I didn't like, I was constantly lying to myself. I was a liar. That was not how I wanted to live my value of truth.

So I owned up to the fact that I wasn't living my value of truth. I owned up to the fact that every day, prior to forgiving myself, I woke up and made the choice to just give away all of my healthy energy in order to protect my precious baggage of guilt and shame. Prior to forgiving myself, every day was like a chess game, as I strategically chose my words and actions not based on authenticity but on making sure no one "found me out"—and I was exhausted by the end of every day.

In order to live my value of truth, I no longer ask myself if I'm authentically showing up to life, being transparent, and always revealing the whole story to everyone else. Instead, I ask if I'm being truthful to myself—because that's the only person who matters. I realized life is a mirror, and the energy frequencies we put into the world are directed right back at us. I realized that if I lived the value of truth for myself, I actually lived it for everyone else at the same time. That was a moment when I started to reclaim my energy. That was a moment that got me closer to naming my purpose in this world.

Mentorship: Providing guidance and development for others

From the start of my career I found myself in pretty significant leadership roles within corporate business. I've always been a go-getter, and businesses appreciate that. In exchange for my efforts, I was given a lot of money, cool titles, and my own office space. I kept delivering what the businesses wanted, and the businesses kept promoting me and giving me status. Sounds great, right? Here's the funny thing: Usually when I joined a business, I would come to the team in a role in which I was working with people day in and day out, from running retail operations to managing strategic teams, and I loved it. Every day I was providing guidance and development for others—mentorship was my sweet spot. I got results from helping other people be their best.

So I kept getting promoted, and I kept saying yes because they kept giving me really great money and titles. The problem was, those promotions landed me in gray cubicle land and required me to work on spreadsheets and go to meetings from 8 a.m. to 5 p.m., where people spent hours talking about the spreadsheets. I think I would rather have chewed on a rusty spoon. Here's where the problem got worse: I was really good at it. I was good at the exact thing that was sucking all of my healthy energy right out of me, so they kept giving me more opportunities to work on more spreadsheets, and I kept getting sucked in because now I was actually making decisions that had a more significant impact on the business. To make matters more difficult, and to make it even harder to break free, they kept paying me more. I left cubicle land every day absolutely drained.

This cycle happened to me three times before I caught on to what was going on. In 2006, I had my moment—the fork in the road. I was laid off, but given a choice: I could stay with the business by taking on a new role, or leave with my severance package. Now, let me be clear. The severance package was not glorious. I was given $4,000, an opportunity to collect unemployment, and a 30-day period to transition out of the business. Due to life circumstances, I had no savings and a whole hell of a lot of bills that maxed out my means. So initially I decided to interview for my next "dream job" within the business, and look elsewhere for another corporate gig.

The interview process was going great, and I was one of the top candidates. I also had a few other opportunities that surfaced at other businesses. The situation was looking good.

Then one morning, I sat with my coffee watching everyone walk into the office. I just sat there and watched everyone walk in like zombies, numb to the world around them. Most worked 12-hour days. Some had to drop their kids off at 7 a.m. and did not pick them up again until 6:30 p.m. People who spent time stressing about what everyone else was going to think about the spreadsheet they created for the morning meeting. People who gave up their dreams for the golden handcuffs. Then it happened. I said it out loud: "Oh my God, that's me! I'm the zombie. I'm the one choosing the golden handcuffs. I'm the one stressing over spreadsheets. I don't want to be a zombie. I don't want to live life as a zombie anymore. I actually want to live life!"

That was the day I decided I was going to hang up my corporate hat in the traditional sense. You see, I love business, but I knew in that moment that working inside in a business of any kind was not going to allow me to honor who I am in a way that actually gave me healthy energy. For some people, being inside a business is exactly what they need to honor their values, and that's great. For me it was not. So I took myself out of my "dream job" interview process, said no to the other opportunities, and started my own business that was all about providing guidance and development for others in business, in a way that was true to who I am.

Let me be clear: Making the jump out of my previous career path wasn't easy. I went through an identity crisis, got depressed, struggled financially, and experienced some significant relationship challenges. Yet I wouldn't trade those experiences for the world. Because now, seven years later, I'm filled with healthy energy because I chose to jump and honor what I valued. I chose to honor my own truth. Now, every morning I get to wake up and know that I'm telling the truth to myself and not living against what I personally value in life. The day I jumped was a moment when I started to reclaim my energy. That was a moment that got me closer to naming my purpose in this world.

Growth: Continuously learning, developing myself, and setting out to achieve without restraint

I used to think I had a problem with a little thing called *maintenance*. It didn't matter if it was in the world of business or in my personal life, the minute something I created fell into maintenance mode my good energy was vacuumed right out of me. I became lethargic and depressed. What would normally take an hour took eight, and procrastination became a daily fight. Even the word *maintenance* felt like nails on a chalkboard. The problem was that my disdain toward the idea of maintenance was causing havoc in my life. I needed to figure this maintenance thing out—or did I?

When I finally named growth as one of my personal values, and could describe what it meant, two things happened. One, I realized that when I heard the word *maintain*, what I heard in my head was, "You need to stop continuously learning, stop developing yourself, and stop setting out to achieve without restraint." The minute that statement came into my head I went into rebellion mode. "Well if that's the case, fine, I'm just not going to do anything." Here's the frustrating part. I knew maintenance was incredibly important. In fact, I wanted maintenance as a personal value—but it's not my value, and that's okay. This realization brought me to the second thing that happened: I took responsibility for what was happening, and I changed.

I started owning the fact that doing maintenance-related activities depleted my energy. Here's the thing: Maintenance itself wasn't depleting my energy; my energy was being depleted because I felt as though I was wasting valuable time on something that had nothing to do with my purpose. Essentially I was right, but I needed to figure out how to change things so I didn't end up in situations that required me to put energy in things that weren't part of my personal values.

I started becoming transparent with people, and asking for their help. I stopped trying to be a round peg in a square hole. Here's the beautiful thing that happened: People started thanking me for being so honest. They told me how impressed they were that I was aware of what did and didn't give me energy, and that I actually honored the commitment I made to myself—that I wouldn't commit to anything unless it was aligned with my values. That was a moment when I started to reclaim my energy. That was a moment that got me closer to naming my purpose in this world.

Renewal: Being a catalyst for change

This was the easiest of my values to start living, because it's just who I am. We all have a value that almost states our purpose out loud. Yours will become obvious once you name all your values. I am a catalyst for change. Everything I do, everything I enjoy, is about experiencing and supporting evolution and change in people and in our world. It's a guarantee that as long as I'm doing something that allows me to be a catalyst for change, I'm in my sphere of healthy energy and everyone around me will benefit.

Once I was able to name my values, I was able to figure out my life purpose, and then I named "it." Not every responsibility that we have in life will always fall within our purpose. For example, I still don't like yard work, I'm not a fan of administrative tasks, and quite frankly I hate having to do laundry—but I do it all because I have to, not because it's my purpose in life. That being said, in time I have been able to align about 90 percent of my life around my values, and I get to wake up looking forward to my day. Yes, I still get tired, but being tired after doing what you love feels drastically different than the tired that comes from doing things that deplete your energy. Just think about the last time you spent hours doing that one thing you love to do. When I finally found my fire truck, life, work, relationships, and everything in between started to become fun again, and I started to put healthy energy back into the world.

My purpose in life is to improve the health and well-being of humanity by making this world a better place to live. I am accomplishing my purpose by living my values: believing in and honoring what is greater than myself, authentically showing up to life, being transparent, and always revealing the whole story. Every day I make sure I'm providing genuine guidance and development to others. Continuously learning, developing myself, and setting out to achieve without restraint. I am a catalyst for change.

How one business put a Values Inquiry into action

Leah is a business analyst in a consumer goods business. Her business just completed the one-month Values Inquiry in which everyone was encouraged to come up with their most significant values. The campaign started with one question showing up on the home page of the intranet: "What are your personal values?" No explanation, just a question. At first Leah was skeptical and thought it was just another employee engagement ploy to get people to work harder. However, the question caught her eye, and she realized she couldn't answer it. *My values? What? I don't know.* She closed the home page and went to her next meeting.

The next morning that same question was still on the home page of the intranet, and when she checked her e-mail, there was a message in her inbox that asked another question: "What moment has been the highlight of your life? Describe it. Why was it a highlight? Who was there? What did the environment look like, feel like, sound like? What words were spoken or written? How did you feel, and why? What value was being respected or honored?" She thought, *Well that's easy. It was when my family actually came to visit after more than three years. It was amazing. My brother even brought his dog. We spent a week just hanging out, camping, and being in nature the way we used to when I was a kid. They all showed up like they said they would—every one of them. I'll never forget it. The smell of the spring dew each morning when we woke up. The burnt coffee that was as thick as mud but tasted so good because we were all in desperate need of caffeine. Now that I think about it, I value relationships and family over everything. If I don't get time with my family, or have meaningful relationships at work, everything else seems like a chore and I have no energy.*

The next day when Leah came into the office, she was actually looking forward to seeing if a new question was in her inbox. And there was. This message had a pretty straightforward subject line: "Who have you told?" She thought, *What?* When she opened the message it simply read, "To whom are you going to tell your values?" She said out loud, "You actually want me to tell someone? I don't think so." She closed her screen and went on with her day.

The next morning, there was a card on her desk. There was a picture on the card of a man who looked really happy. It was cheesy and it actually made her laugh out loud. She thought to herself, *Laughing is always a good way to start my day.* When she opened the card, the message read, "Ask someone what his or her values are today." She thought, *Okay, these people aren't giving up.*

That day she went to lunch with her friend Patrick. During the conversation, she remembered the card and thought, *What the hell.* She asked Patrick if he had received the card. His response was simply, "Yep, I received the card." A little annoyed, Leah continued with, "Are you going to share what your values are?" Patrick gave her a strange look and then started to share his values. It turned into a 30-minute conversation. On the way back to their desks, Leah and Patrick both commented on what a great conversation they had, and wondered if they were going to get another card tomorrow.

The next day, there was a question posted on the parking ramp. The same question was on the intranet: "What does it look like?" She thought, *What do mean, "What does it look like?" It's a value, not an experience.* When she opened her e-mail, there was a message with the subject line, "No, really, what does it look like?" When Leah opened the message, the question was more detailed: "What does your value look like, feel like, and sound like? If your value was played out in a movie, what would be the plot?" Now this question got Leah. All day she was thinking about the question. She even went to bed thinking about the question and came up with movie plot before she fell asleep.

On Friday Leah was excited to share her movie plot with Patrick. She had even named him as one of her characters. She was very impressed with herself. As she was walking to her desk, she saw a few people walking around with flip cams. She thought, *What's this all about? And how can I get to my desk as fast as humanly possible without anyone seeing me slide by?* As she tried to walk past the flip-cam people, she got busted. One of the women from the marketing team came up to her and said, "Hey, Leah, do you mind if we ask you a quick question?" Leah said, "Sure," even though she was thinking, *They always say that, but it's never quick.*

Before Leah really knew what was happening, the flip cam was on and she was being interviewed. She thought, *I knew this wasn't going to be quick. Did this really have to happen on the morning I chose not to wear any makeup?* The woman from the marketing team asked Leah about her reaction to this week's values experience. Leah shared her initial reaction and a little bit about the great conversation she and Patrick had had over lunch. Than the woman said, "Can you share your value? Did you come up with a movie plot?" Leah was actually pretty impressed with her movie plot, so she started answering the question and even forgot she was being filmed. "I decided to base the movie on the top two values I discovered this week: family and commitment. The movie takes place on Ozar, a planet that is in desperate need of an alternative food supply, or nutrient-filled soil that will allow them to grow healthy food. Oparc and Delian, two natives, decide to leave the planet in search for a solution, each committing to their families that they would return home safe. The story is about their adventures, and how their values of family and commitment impacted their loyalty to one another and their drive to keep each other safe at all costs. Every decision they made was influenced by these two values that helped them persevere and defeat danger every step of the way."

The woman was impressed, and asked, "Given that amazing movie plot, how are you going to start living your value of family and commitment here at work?" Leah gave her a surprised look and said, "Wow, that's a good question. I guess I'm going to start remembering that the people I work with every day are kind of like a family. And if I start treating them with the same level of appreciation, I may actually enjoy working with them even more than I do right now. As far as commitment goes, I'm going to make sure I let people know how important that value is to me. That showing up to meetings on time and doing what they say they will means the world to me. Just being around people who keep their word gives me energy and makes me want to be here." The woman gave her a smile and said, "That's a wrap. Thank you so much being part of the experience, Leah. Keep your eye out. The video footage will be up on the intranet on Monday."

Sure enough, Monday morning came around and the videos where up on the intranet. The marketing team had captured more than 50 videos that day. To Leah's surprise, they were all pretty good. Some of the movie plots were amazing (but she still thought hers was the best). That Monday, the questions started again, but this time there was more of a buzz in the air. Everyone was talking about the videos. People were being more open with their values, and actually having fun with the process.

During the third week, every team had an outing of some sort. Some went to lunch, some did a happy hour, and some had a fun gathering in the office. During the outing, teams talked about the experience, shared their values with each other, and voted on the best movie plot. The fourth week included an opportunity to meet with the executive leaders, and everyone was able to share with the leader their personal values, why their values were important, and how they plan on living their values in the business as a way to re-fuel their energy. The leaders shared their values too, and for many people, it was the first time the leaders actually appeared human.

Everyone appreciated that the business put so much energy into the Values Inquiry experience, and that the experience was truly for and about the people who made up the business. For the first time, everyone felt that the business leaders actually made people a priority over financial results, and they were excited to find out what was next.

The Credo

The second phase of the Performance Through Purpose cam-paign is called the Credo. This is a three-month experience during which people put all their values together, name their purpose, and make a commitment to start honoring them. At the end of the three-month experience, every person in the business will have a personal credo, a clearly defined plan of action on how they're going to align their life with their values, and be able to talk about how they're going to start showing up to the world in a way that gives them healthy energy.

During the first month, everyone in the business creates and posts their written credo along with their picture online. Teams share their credo statements with each other, giving encouragement and helping each other craft the right language. Each team then creates videos of people sharing their value stories. These are the stories, similar to the examples I provided earlier, that illustrate how people knew what values were important to them and why. The stories are posted online.

During the second and third month, everyone in the business creates their alignment plan, a clearly defined plan of action on how they will align their life with their values. Some businesses may choose to create a private page on their intranet for teams to post plans, share ideas, and support each other, similar to the online discussion board idea presented in Chapter 2.

This is not an easy process for people to go through, and they will need support. The business needs to provide people with mentors or trained practitioners who can ask them the right questions, challenge them, and make sure they remain true to themselves during the process. If your leaders are functional, they may be the right people for this role. If they're not functional, you'll need to hire people who are.

At the end of the third month, when people feel good about their credo and alignment plan, everyone in the business makes a video that is a public declaration of their credo, and how they will live their values and honor themselves in order to get healthy energy back into their lives, so they can start putting healthy energy back into the world. The video is then posted on the intranet. Here's an example of a personal credo. Each declaration will follow the same format.

Personal Credo

My purpose in life is to improve the health and wellbeing of humanity by making this world a better place to live. I am accomplishing my purpose by living my values of:

Spirituality: Believing in and honoring what is greater than myself.

Going forward I will...

Truth: Authentically showing up to life, being transparent, and always revealing the whole story.

Going forward I will...

Mentorship: Providing genuine guidance and development to others.

Going forward I will...

Growth: Continuously learning, developing myself, and setting out to achieve without restraint.

Going forward I will...

Renewal: I am a catalyst for change.

Going forward I will...

Living "It" Out Loud

This is the final phase of the campaign, and begins only after everyone in the business has successfully created their alignment plan and posted their personal declaration video. Living "It" Out Loud is an eight-month process, acknowledging that people have eight chakra systems that need to be cleared from toxic energy and balanced so they can reclaim their healthy energy and contribute it to the business ecosystem. The outcome of the experience is that people live their declaration with the support of the business. Each employee receives two energy sessions per month by a trained practitioner (16 total), alignment plans become integrated into business-as-usual activity, and on the eighth month the campaign ends with a celebration that acknowledges everyone's hard work and progress.

Energy Work

In order to live "it" out loud, people need help healing the energy they have and replenishing their system with healthy energy. People need to learn how to manage and protect their personal energy. As discussed in Chapter 1, energy work influences the flow of energy though our bodies, positively impacting our thoughts, emotions, and actions. The regular practice of energy work improves personal energy flow, reduces exhaustion, increases our productivity, and allows us to be vulnerable—creating the opportunity to experience transformative growth and begin living a high-character life. In order for your energy ecosystem to be fully operable everyone in your business needs to become functional. This book has addressed leaders first, because it's the leaders who model the way for everyone else in the business, but ultimately everyone needs to be functional if you want the energy system to work.

Alignment Plans

During this stage, alignment plans are created (how people plan to live their credo within the business going forward), and alignment teams are provided for support. These teams are made up of various people from various areas of the business. Teams meet monthly, and the intent of each meeting is for people to share how they're integrating the alignment plan into their lives. The conversation gives people the opportunity to talk about challenges, celebrate successes, and support each other along the eight-month journey.

Everyone in the business has the responsibility to meet with their direct leader monthly to seek support and guidance in an effort to integrate the alignment plan into business-as-usual activity. Alignment plans may initiate job changes, reallocation of role assignments, and/or add additional initiatives to team strategies. It's the responsibility of the leader to be open to change, support everyone on the team, and help people think of creative ways to move their alignment plan forward in the business.

A critical component of the process is a predetermined leadership committee made up of eight functional leaders from different areas of the business. This committee is specifically created to mitigate potential challenges caused by leaders who are not modeling functional behaviors. The committee is given the authority to intervene and support people when necessary. People are encouraged to go directly to the committee if they experience challenges with their direct leader.

Celebration

Once the 12-month Performance Through Purpose Campaign is complete, it's time to celebrate. People deserve to be acknowledged for all the hard work they've put into changing their lives in order to reclaim healthy energy. They deserve to be recognized for their amazing progress and willingness to be part of something new and different. This is when people get to share their success stories with the entire business. This is when people get to celebrate themselves. The business can choose how to celebrate people at the end of the process; it may be a large event or a special gathering for alignment teams. Whatever the celebration, make it count! And don't forget to archive the experience. It's always filled with healthy energy that's worth saving.

Chapter Highlights

* **People are driven to live out a purpose.**

* "I want to spread my wings and fly, be part of something greater than myself, and feel as though I'm living my purpose." This is the voice of Principle #4. Sitting within the thymus chakra of your business, this energy center is driven by creating opportunity for people to become engaged in the business, on their terms.

* The idea of purpose often gets confused with the idea that people should be looking for something tangible. They say things like, "I'm looking for *it*. I can't find *it*. What is *it*?" But it's not an *it*. Purpose is not a noun. Purpose is a verb. Your purpose shows up in how you show up to live your life. It's not a thing that's waiting to be found.

✳ When your business helps people live their purpose, people want to help your business live its purpose.

✳ Values are how we name what we find important, and what gives us energy. Like the flour and eggs that help a cake become a cake, values are the ingredients that make up our purpose.

✳ To successfully build a healthy energy ecosystem, you must create both opportunity to discover and flexibility to live out the discovery.

✳ The Performance Through Purpose Campaign helps everyone in the business identify their true life purpose, and gives people the opportunity to live their purpose in the business. The campaign is based on three core experiences: the **Values Inquiry**, the **Credo**, and **Living "It" Out Loud**.

✳ If your leaders aren't yet functional, leadership functionality needs to be the first priority. The crown chakra of your business needs to be flowing with healthy energy before the business can even hope to have its thymus chakra free from toxic energy.

Principle #5

Freedom Turns Ideas and Vision Into Reality

Principle #5 sits within the heart chakra of the business. The heart chakra is balanced with trust, compassion, and freedom. This is one of the most important business chakras—the easiest to identify, but by far the most difficult to balance. The health of your business's heart chakra shows up in the attitude of the business, often referred to as its internal brand. You can walk into a place of business and immediately feel if its heart chakra is toxic. The heart chakra is where people become emotionally connected to the business, and if this chakra is contaminated with toxic energy, people automatically become apathetic, disengaged, and resistant to any type of change, no matter how small.

The heart chakra of your business must be clear, balanced, and circulating healthy energy if you have any desire for innovation. If it's not clear, turning ideas and vision into reality becomes increasingly more difficult. You can design the best plan in the world, build the best business systems, and hire the best innovative talent, but if the heart chakra is clogged your efforts will be stalled.

You see, the heart of the business is just like the heart of a human—I mean that soulfully. When people feel they are genuinely able to give and receive trust and compassion, they have no problem opening their heart and wearing it on their sleeve. When trust and compassion exist people actually want to help and support other people around them. Just like the heart chakra of a human, the heart chakra of a business will only remain open if people feel they have the genuine freedom to create, to be, and to show all of themselves without having to worry about suffering from consequences that create fear and shame.

The result of a healthy heart chakra in a business is innovation and a great attitude/internal brand. When people feel free, and are rooted in trust and compassion, they can't help but feel good, want to create, surface new ideas, think outside the box, and do everything they can to help bring the vision to reality. If you want innovation, if you want to turn ideas and vision into reality, and if you want people to have a great attitude, then you want a heart chakra that circulates healthy energy throughout the business.

The recipe is easy: Create an environment that makes people feel safe and protected from emotional harm. Build trust between every person who is part of the business, and make sure everyone walks the way of compassion. You do those three things, and your business will no doubt have a strong internal brand that masters the art of turning ideas and vision into reality.

Innovation

I've never met a business leader who didn't talk about the need for innovation. Most leaders understand that innovation is what creates progress, and progress is how businesses get results. That being said, there's a dichotomy between what many leaders say they want and how they actually run their business. They want new ideas from people, but they themselves create a prescriptive environment where people are restricted from creating and moving forward. They want a culture that thrives on good attitude, but they themselves show up with a bad attitude. They want collaboration, but they take no time themselves to build trust. They want the business to be seen by the public as socially responsible, but they themselves show no heart, and lack compassion in the eyes of the people working for the business. You see, you can't have it both ways. You can't have an innovative business that turns ideas and vision into reality, and choose to model characteristics that derail innovation—you're either all in or all out. You need to make a choice. If you're all in, you need to own it all the way.

We can't talk about innovation without reflecting on Einstein's quote: "Everything is energy and that's all there is to it. Match the frequency of the reality you want, and you cannot help but get that reality. It can be no other way. This is not philosophy. This is physics." In other words, you get back what you give. It's the basic law of attraction. And you can physically see it happen in business day in and day out. If a business wants to be innovative, and if it wants an internal brand that represents a great attitude, then the people running the business need to authentically model the characteristics that create innovation and a great attitude—trust, compassion, and freedom.

If the leaders aren't modeling trust, compassion, and freedom, the business will just keep producing more of the dysfunction leaders are choosing to model, and the desire to have true innovation and a healthy internal brand will never be reached. Sam saw this reality play out after taking over as senior VP of human capital for an international agricultural business that has more than 250,000 people working throughout the United States and Europe. For the past 10 years, the business has grown by leaps and bounds, but has gained a reputation for having a difficult work environment. The business hasn't appeared to respect work-life balance. People on salary have been expected to work weekends and evenings, regardless of personal commitments, in an effort to "get the job done." Frustration has brewed due to endless projects finding homes in the document graveyard. Leaders have been spending their time appeasing higher-ups and playing politics rather than focusing on truly leading teams. The environment is prescriptive, causing people to be hesitant to surface new ideas unless directed to do so by senior management. Even senior-level leaders often feel as though they've become task masters.

The CEO asked Sam to join the business three years ago when he saw the need for the business to become more innovative. The CEO knew that to continue leading the industry, the business needed to begin surfacing marketplace solutions that could pave the way for growth throughout the next 10 years. Sam's charge was to "Fix the culture, get people engaged, and create an environment of innovation." No small feat.

So Sam did what many leaders in that position would do: Sam brought the Human Capital team and relevant senior leaders together for a two-day offsite strategy session. Their aim was to create a three-year plan to increase innovation. Outside speakers were brought in to inspire creative thinking. The offsite location was contemporary, with lots of natural light, and they had every type of kinesthetic learning object at their fingertips. The team was ready to be innovative and create a plan that would work.

At the end of the two-day session, everyone felt great about their plan. It was fairly simple, and revolved around the typical human capital functions, including **engagement**, **communications**, and

leadership development. Engagement was first on the list because the business continuously had mediocre engagement scores. The plan required all leaders in the business to develop an individual action plan that would improve their respective teams' engagement scores. These action plans were to be communicated to senior management, and engagement scores would be included on every leader's annual review. The goal was to increase engagement levels by 15 percent.

Internal communication efforts were the second priority within the three-year strategy. The team knew that people needed to become more emotionally invested in the business if the culture was going to improve, so they created an "attitude campaign." The campaign was intended to show that the business had heart by surfacing evidence that compassion was alive and well throughout the business. The campaign included videos and collateral that highlighted how people's roles mattered to the business. All internal communication would be positioned around the campaign, and the new campaign vernacular would now be used in team meetings and leadership communication. The internal communication strategy had a direct tie to engagement.

The third and last element of the strategy was leadership development. In an effort to lead the innovation movement forward, every leader would go though a distinct training series. The series consisted of workshops designed to teach leaders at all levels different innovation techniques to use with teams, and a culture model that was proven to work across industries. Both the strategy team and C-suite leaders were thrilled with the strategy—it was well-thought-out and seemed to project realistic yet promising results. Ready, set, and go.

Six months into the strategy, everything was going well and the team was feeling good. Deliverables were met on time, the strategy team remained committed, and the C-suite seemed satisfied with the tangible outcomes that were being produced. The first group of leaders had started the training series, every leader was in the process of creating their engagement action plan, and evidence of the new communication campaign was everywhere in the business. Sam was feeling amazingly good about the strategy team's performance.

When the team hit the 18-month mark, questions started to surface. Why did the environment almost feel worse now than when the team launched the strategy? Engagement scores remained mediocre—in fact, some areas decreased. The attitude campaign became wall art and letterhead. Leaders shared what they learned in the innovation workshop during team meetings, but the practice of the innovation techniques seemed to disappear as quickly as the workshop experience. Culture was not better.

The team stayed the course, knowing that culture and engagement were not things that would change overnight. After two years of less-than-stellar results, modifications were made and a few recognition events and humanitarian committees were added. The team hired an outside consulting firm to help devise a more comprehensive approach to the culture change. Three years went by and the business achieved moderate results at best, but nowhere near the results the team projected or what the business needed to do in order to sustain its position as an industry leader and continue surfacing marketplace solutions that could pave the way for growth throughout the next 10 years. The C-suite, Sam, and the entire strategy team all had the same question: What's next?

Sam's approach to creating a more innovative business and improving the culture was no different from what most businesses do. In fact, in nearly two decades, I've seen the same scenario play out an endless number of times. Sure, terminology has changed, but the essence of what businesses are trying to become remains exactly the same, as do the challenges that are causing the performance blockages. In every scenario the same things are always missing: **trust**, **compassion**, and **freedom**. The business puts all its energy into creating a strategic plan, with all the necessary tactics. As a result, the plan looks great on paper—and *only* on paper. There is no energy put toward creating an environment rooted in trust, compassion, and freedom. There's no energy put toward emotionally connecting with people. Even if the plan *appears* to emotionally connect to people, if the people leading the business are not emotionally connected to everyone else in the business by way of trust, compassion, and freedom, the business won't get the desired results.

If you look at Sam's story, the question of "What's next?" becomes easy to answer. We know the business hasn't appeared to respect work-life balance. If the CEO really wants innovation, to change the culture for the better, and for people to be more engaged, the CEO needs to ask a different question: How can the business get all of its leaders, regardless of their level, living the way of trust, compassion, and freedom? Now that's a strategy that would work.

Whenever I'm facilitating a strategy session or working with groups of leaders on ways they can become more innovative and improve the culture, they usually want to spend a great deal of time telling me all the reasons why they're frustrated with the lack of results they've experienced thus far. Most business leaders have gone down a similar road to Sam's, and they've spent a countless amount of hours "assessing" the problem. I always enjoy listening, and I always wait until they're completely done telling me the whole story before I respond. I wait, because the story always ends with the same statement and question: "Here's where you come in. What do we do next?"

My response is always the same. Sometimes it's more colorful and elaborate, but regardless of the leadership team, my response is always, "I know exactly why your business isn't getting the results you want in the timeframe you want. And I have the solution. It's guaranteed to work. It's low cost. And you'll get the immediate results you're looking for—again, guaranteed." At this point, I have their attention. Some people laugh. Most people grab their pens and get ready to take notes. I tell them what they need to do: "Tonight, on your way home from the office, each of you needs to stop at the store and buy one thing: a mirror." At that point the room always becomes silent. I usually wait at least 30 seconds, and let everyone sit in silence before I start talking again. Then I keep going. "You see, you are a direct reflection of your business and all of the people within it, and the business and all of the people within it are a direct reflection of you. If your business isn't 'working,' or your people aren't responding, *you're the problem*—bottom line. Now you have a choice. You can either own the reality that you're the problem, or you can avoid it. It's your choice, but I will tell you that owning it costs a hell of a lot less, and it's a hell of a lot more successful than avoidance."

I always end with one question, and I don't talk again until everyone in the room answers it: "Which is it, ownership or avoidance?" Every once in a while I'll have a leader actually stand up and walk out—a direct indication that he is suffering from dysfunctional leadership disease, and *he* is at the core of why the business isn't performing and why unhealthy energy is running rampant. Most often, the room answers the question with another question: "What does 'owning it' mean, exactly?" That's when I know it's game time.

There is one other scenario that sometimes plays out: denial. Some businesses have what I call a numb heart chakra. The heart chakra is toxic, and is circulating enough unhealthy energy to take down a city, yet the leaders of the business, collectively, are convinced there is nothing wrong. They're still asking for help with innovation, and they still want a healthy internal brand, but they refuse to admit, or face the fact, that they will never get the results they want until they figure out how to get functional, and walk the way of trust, compassion, and freedom. If this is you or your business, I recommend that you again take the Leadership Functionality Quiz in Chapter 1. You will be unable to move forward and build a healthy energy ecosystem for your business unless you have a leadership team willing to "own it." You see, the heart chakra of a business is just like the heart of a human: The heart always knows the truth, and denial is simply unhealthy protection put in place by the fear of facing reality. And just like a human, when the business is finally willing to face the fear and "own it," it can move forward.

Trust

Trust is being able to express yourself freely, openly, and without hesitation, because you feel protected and safe from having to experience shame, physical harm, hurt, or guilt. Now think about the people in your life. Using this definition of trust, where do people in your life fall on your trust curve? We all have a trust curve, and we put everyone we know somewhere on it. That also means you're on everyone else's trust curve.

At the beginning of any interaction most people put others at the bottom of their trust curve, indicating that trust, in most people's minds, is earned. Then, through "feel good" experiences, you move people up your trust curve. The more you feel able to express yourself freely, openly, and without hesitation, because you feel protected and safe when you're around that person, that person may even make it to the top of your trust curve—these are the people you would do whatever it takes to help, support, and ensure their success. It feels amazing when you're at the top of someone's trust curve, and it feels unbelievably fantastic when two people are at the top of each others' trust curve simultaneously—the ultimate relationship of any kind. The people at the top of our trust curve are the people who fuel us with healthy energy, and who receive healthy energy from us.

The opposite is also true. We all have people in our lives whom we don't feel safe and protected around when it comes to expressing ourselves freely, openly, and without hesitation. We have people in our lives who stir the fear of shame, physical harm, hurt, or guilt within us. These people are at the bottom of our trust curve, and we are cautious, consciously or subconsciously, about doing anything for these people. These are the people who deplete our good energy, fill us with toxic energy, and receive unhealthy energy from us.

People's trust curves go with them everywhere. There are no exceptions, especially in business. Businesses that have a healthy energy ecosystem are placed high on people's trust curve. The higher the business is placed on an individual's trust curve, the better the energy. There's a direct correlation. The goal of the business should always be optimal placement on everyone's trust curve, because then, and only then, are people expressing their ideas freely, openly, and without hesitation. Then and only then, the internal brand is thriving with a positive attitude and innovation is an attainable destination for the business.

Compassion

You can't have trust without compassion. It's a guarantee that if someone doesn't see you as a compassionate human being, you are not high on his or her personal trust curve. It's not possible because compassion is about genuinely empathizing with others, and showing sympathy with authenticity—both compassionate actions that result in trust. Compassion breeds trust, respect, and loyalty throughout the business, and shows everyone that the business has heart. When leaders have compassion, it's evident that they care about how the business impacts people and communities. Compassion heightens engagement, retains the best talent, and circulates healthy energy throughout the business. Compassion is at the core of trust.

Compassion is an action word; it's a verb. If the business has compassion publicly noted as one of its core values, everyone *will* expect every leader to *show* compassion in everything they do. If leaders don't, the business has created a breeding ground for hurt, anger, and disappointment, resulting in energetic green slime everywhere. If the business states that it values compassion, leaders at all levels better be able to authentically show acts of compassion. If leaders are unable to match their words and the value labels they put out into the business, people will have no desire to do anything except the bare minimum required to collect a paycheck. And when the opportunity arises, people will jump at the chance to leave the business and work someplace where leaders actually have the ability to show compassion.

Some businesses say, "We have chosen the values we aspire to attain. Our values are goals for how we want to live in the future. It's important that our values show that we are trying to change." Here's the deal: That may be the intent of the values you've chosen for your business, but if every leader can't live up to the values you've publicly stated, your business will find itself constantly battling culture, engagement, and retention deficiency.

That being said, it's great that so many businesses have compassion as a value; every business should. The problem is not in naming compassion as a value. The problem is that businesses are looking at the value of compassion as aspirational, rather than a required behavior every leader is expected to live and is furthermore held accountable to living.

Freedom

Freedom is what turns ideas and vision into reality. True freedom is only possible when trust and compassion are present—there's no other way.

From government to business, the word *freedom* automatically evokes emotion and creates action. If freedom is taken away, it creates the action of rebellious destruction—silently or out loud. When genuinely given, freedom creates fluidity and the ability to act and create independently. If you want the heart chakra of your business to circulate healthy energy, and you want a business in which people generate new ideas and show up with a good attitude, then freedom needs to be a foundational operating principle for your business.

Giving people freedom means letting them express themselves freely, openly, and without hesitation. True freedom comes with a feeling of being protected and safe from having to experience shame, physical harm, hurt, or guilt. From small mom-and-pop shops to large international conglomerates, business wars for freedom are being waged every day. People want freedom, and many leaders are fearful of relinquishing control. The battle can become fierce enough that it's like World War III is erupting in the workplace. The difference in business is that people can't always see the war happening with their eyes; they can only feel it, and they don't even know it's a war. They call this war *business-as-usual activity*.

I love that statement—*business-as-usual activity*. I think it's my favorite dysfunctional thing I hear leaders say. "We want performance. We want people to be energized and engaged. We want to be innovative. We want people to show up with a great attitude. But we want it in our traditional, prescriptive, hierarchical culture that's rooted in standard operating processes that are designed to keep the machine moving. That's how good businesses are run, and how lots of money is made. Change is good, as long as it fits within our business-as-usual activity." Uh, hello? KNOCK KNOCK. Is anyone home? You can't have what you're saying you want in the traditional, prescriptive, hierarchical culture you've created. It's not possible. That's like telling a nation of people they're free, getting their hopes up, creating an excitement that they can finally breathe again, and then turning around and taking all their rights away. "Oh, just joking. You didn't think we were actually going to change the way we do things, did you? Oops. No. We didn't like that idea. It didn't fit into our comfort zone. Sorry. But if you have any ideas that fit directly inside our box we'll consider the possibility." Now the business has one or thousands of people who are angry birds dumping toxic energetic green slime into the business. Or worse, the business now has one or thousands of apathetic people who really don't care what happens to the business as long as they keep getting paid. People's thoughts and emotions start creating energy that takes the form of silent but deadly arsenic being pumped into the business, and the business gets exactly what it wanted: business-as-usual activity.

Remember Business Principle #4? *People are driven to live out a purpose.* People perform when they can spread their wings and fly. People want to be free to live their purpose in this world, and when they do, there's nothing they can't accomplish. When they do, your business benefits tenfold. Freedom is the essence of who we are as human beings, regardless of our environment. Freedom is the answer to the question Sam was asking. Freedom is the answer to the question, "How does our business become innovative and create a healthy culture where people want to work and want to be engaged?" Freedom is what's next. It's freedom a business needs to give, embrace, and live if it wants innovation and energy. Freedom is what turns ideas and vision into reality, and it's what will drive profits for your business in the future. Without giving people freedom, your business won't be able to achieve healthy energy and innovation. The only way your business will attain freedom is if your leaders are functional and clearly understand how to give permission and protection.

As we've discussed, leadership functionality is what needs to come first. The energetic health of your leaders is *the* most important priority of your business and its financial success—period. It doesn't matter if you're the CEO of a billion-dollar company or the owner of an ice-cream shop, the only way your business will become innovative and drive profits while circulating healthy energy is if you own the fact that you and all the leaders in the business need to become functional. Furthermore, the only way leadership functionality can happen is if you and all the leaders in the business own the fact that *you're all currently dysfunctional.* That's step one: awareness. Choose to own the fact that you're dysfunctional. Choose to own the fact that your leadership dysfunction is the reason your business isn't achieving exactly what it wants to achieve. Choose to own the fact that your fear of letting go of control, power, and money is the reason why you're not giving people the freedom they need to move your business forward. Own it, and then have the courage to choose to do whatever it takes to get functional. If you're questioning whether leadership functionality is even an issue for you or your business, go back to Chapter 1 and take the quiz. The process of attaining leadership functionality, modeling high-character values, and helping to circulate healthy energy throughout the business is also outlined at the end of that chapter.

Again, owning leadership functionality is your first priority if you want people to surface new ideas, if you want a culture that thrives on a good attitude, if you want collaboration, and if you want the business to be seen by the public as socially responsible—all characteristics of an energetically healthy business that succeeds at innovation. You can't have an innovative business that turns ideas and vision into reality when leaders choose to model characteristics that derail innovation—you're either all in or all out. You need to make a choice. If you're all in, you need to own it all the way. And owning it means you that you need to take a good solid look in the mirror, name your dysfunction, admit that you're the problem, and then make a choice to get energetically healthy.

Permission is the second element of freedom, and is the act of giving people consent to make decisions, exercise good judgment, and express viewpoints and ideas openly. Giving permission is how the business becomes fueled with good energy. In Chapter 4, we saw that people want permission to spread their wings and fly. When they feel free to do so, there's nothing they can't accomplish. In business, because of the structures and systems we've created, people need to hear from the leaders of the business that they have permission to move forward in their own way. Even if you are a leader who naturally gives people permission, don't assume that people don't need to hear the words—they do.

Now here's the challenge. Yes, everyone wants and needs freedom. And yes, giving everyone freedom in business is how ideas and vision become reality. That being said, people will resist the freedom you're trying to give them. So this permission/freedom thing is going to be work for the leaders of the business. People want the permission to make decisions freely, but when it's granted, they will get scared of potential repercussions, and their actions will ask for their freedom to be taken away again. It's similar to someone who gets released after being in the penitentiary for 20 years, and intentionally does something wrong in order to get back behind bars—it's because of fear of the unknown. Even though freedom gives people what they want, and freedom is how healthy energy in a business is accomplished, once people have it, they will become afraid of the new responsibility. People will fear failing, repercussions, and the unknown. To most people the thought of failing, and the thought of the unknown, is a thousand times scarier than the thought of remaining behind bars unable to ever spread their wings and fly. If your business is going to benefit from creating an operating model based on giving people freedom, the leaders have no choice but to extend protection.

Protection is the third element of freedom. Protection simply means that you follow through on the permission you've given people to do their job in their own unique way. Protection means that you allow people to experience mistakes as learning opportunities, rather than delivering harsh consequences when things don't go exactly as planned. Protection is about supporting people, and trusting that they'll get to the destination even if they get there differently from how you would have done it. Protection means that leaders take the time to mentor and coach people rather than just jumping in and fixing, changing, and doing people's jobs for them. Protection is the last element of freedom, because it's the action that brings leadership functionality and permission to life.

The reason why leadership functionality is critical to Business Principle #5 is that in order for freedom to exist, every leader must be able to model high-character values. When you grant permission, initially people will get excited, but will inevitably come back to expecting you to answer the question, give them a roadmap, and take charge. At first, people will have no idea how to handle freedom. Leaders have to be healthy enough to patiently ask questions, reinforce that they believe people have the skills and ability to make decisions, provide unwavering support in the form of mentoring and coaching, and exercise restraint so they don't just jump in and try to fix problems or go back on their promise of freedom. If leaders fail to protect, and go back on their promise of freedom, the energy in your business will become worse than when you started.

It's going to take at least 90 days of every leader physically showing high-character values and functional leadership skills for people to even begin to trust that this "freedom thing" is real and not just another flavor of the month. It's going to take at least 90 days for people to begin believing that it's actually okay to freely take care of their part of the business and surface new ideas without suffering harsh repercussions from higher-ups. It will take at least 90 days for the idea of freedom to start becoming an accepted concept in your business, because it's going to take time for people to start feeling as though they can actually express themselves freely, openly, and without hesitation, and feel protected and safe from having to experience shame, physical harm, hurt, or guilt if they mess up. In some businesses, freedom will take much longer than 90 days, because the timeframe is contingent on how toxic the energy of the business was when the freedom process started.

The Process: The Trust Curve Assessment

Freedom turns ideas and vision into reality. A business can only have an operating model based on freedom if the business is high on everyone's trust curve. There's no other way. If people don't trust the business or their leader, then people will have no motivation to accomplish anything beyond the minimum requirement. The goal of the business should always be optimal placement on everyone's trust curve, because then and only then are people expressing their ideas freely, openly, and without hesitation. Then and only then, the internal brand is thriving with a positive attitude and innovation is an attainable destination for the business. Trust is the only way people will emotionally connect to anything the business wants to accomplish.

The first step in establishing business-wide trust is to find out where the business is on the collective trust curve. To do that, you need to administer a trust curve assessment to everyone in the business. The assessment comprises 12 statements, each of which receives a percentage (0–100 percent) as a response. The response percentages are then averaged, and the average percentage is where your business is on the trust curve. The assessment needs to be delivered to everyone in the business regardless of role, and the results must be posted publicly on the intranet or another business-wide communication system. This is not a "behind closed doors, and only revealed if the results are good" assessment.

The following are the 12 trust curve statements. The platform question is simply, "What percentage of time are these statements true?"

1. My leader's behaviors help me feel as though I can express my ideas freely, openly, and without hesitation.

2. The business's processes and systems help me to feel as though I can express my ideas freely, openly, and without hesitation.

3. What my leader tells me is always true.

4. The information the business communicates is always true.

5. My leader and the business have my best interests in mind anytime decisions are made.

6. My leader listens to me, and I know my leader hears what I say because he or she responds with genuine questions, comments, or beneficial concerns.

7. My leader and the business always make me feel supported, and help me to know that I add value. I know this to be true because following up with commitments made is a priority that is always attained.

8. The business environment allows me to freely make decisions, take care of clients, and implement new ideas in my own unique way.

9. Every leader in the business shows compassion. The business leaders genuinely empathize with others and show sympathy with authenticity.

10. The business environment makes me feel safe and protected emotionally; I completely trust that my leader's response to my ideas will not cause me to feel shame, hurt, or guilt.

11. The business environment makes me feel safe and protected physically.

12. I trust that I can be my true self within the business, and that all leaders and peers genuinely respect my true self in the business.

Here's the deal: If you want to know how to improve trust in your business, people will tell you, and they will be right. It's amazing. The people in your business are brilliant—that's why you hired them. They know exactly what the business and its leaders need to do right now in order to move up the trust curve.

Here's the twist, and the change from business-as-usual activity: The next step in the process is for the people who make up your business to create a trust curve action plan that all the leaders in the business will be expected to follow. Additionally, the business needs to add the *collective* trust curve assessment score to each leader's annual review, the score having a direct impact on each leader's personal financial gain. The key term there is *collective*: The score every leader is held accountable to is a collective trust curve score, not an individual leadership score. This means that if one leader in the business chooses behaviors that take the business down the trust curve, every leader goes down with him—no exceptions. This is what you call collective responsibility (a concept that will be addressed in upcoming chapters). The trust curve assessment process opens the heart chakra of the business so healthy energy can begin circulating.

Proof Point Leadership

Proof point leadership is a concept designed to fuel freedom *after* the business has successfully established trust. Trying to do proof point leadership first will not work. If the trust assessment score is low, then any effort to visibly show that leaders care and have compassion will be seen as lip service and another engagement ploy—filling the business with toxic energy. When done right, and only after trust is built, the proof point leadership concept will energize people, ignite action, and drive profits authentically.

Proof point leadership is how you show people evidence that leaders actually care and have compassion. The technique makes visible the fact that leaders are taking the idea of trust seriously, and that they understand compassion is not just something you talk about. The concept shows proof that leaders are living their promise of giving people freedom to turn ideas and vision into reality. Proof point leadership brings to life a new attitude, a healthy internal brand, and a sense of pride and loyalty among everyone in the business. Proof point leadership makes sure the heart chakra stays open and the business remains healthy, productive, and energetically profitable.

There are three parts to the proof point leadership concept:

1. Capture the moment.

2. Take it viral.

3. Make it mean something.

The concept is done best when using an online platform such as an intranet or dedicated external Website. Gone are the days of the hard-copy newsletter. With YouTube and free Websites at your fingertips there's no reason businesses shouldn't be online. Let's explore all three parts.

Capture the Moment

Everyone in the business is encouraged to capture leaders showing compassion and exercising the principle of giving freedom in great ways. The intent is for the business to be filled with stories and imagery of what true compassion looks like and feels like, and how compassion fuels healthy energy throughout the business. These are not scripted stories. The proof point leadership concept is intentionally designed to be an organic, groundswell occurrence. Yes, you need to create an opportunity for people to capture the moments, and provide resources where necessary, but the minute you turn this into another structured session, or try to write formulated articles that correspond to a communication plan, people will assume ill intent.

People can capture their stories through video, blogs, commenting on blogs, posting relevant articles, and uploading pictures. The intent is to create an online community where compassion and freedom come to life. The only true guideline is that the moments captured must exhibit leaders who are demonstrating compassion in ways that are building trust, giving freedom, and circulating healthy energy throughout the business. Here's the nuance: Everyone in your business can be a leader. *Leadership is an attitude, not a position or title.* Some of the best leaders are those who have led teams forward without ever receiving a title. Capturing the moment is about telling the story of leaders throughout the business who understand and live the true attributes that will energetically move a healthy business forward.

Take It Viral

The goal is for the stories to be so good that they all go viral. Everyone who contributes a story is encouraged to also pass the story on to five additional people, who are then asked to pass the story to five more people, and so on. The intent is for all of the stories to land in the lap of every person in the business.

Make It Mean Something

Saying *thank you* consistently, and with authenticity, is an automatic way of turning toxic energy into healthy energy. The easiest way to start showing compassion, building trust, and helping people feel safe and protected to exercise freedom is by saying thank you. It's amazing to me how many people in the world fail to say thank you. **Make it mean something** is about letting people know how thankful you are for the compassion they're showing, trust they're building, and freedom they're giving. **Make it mean something** is about gratitude. The beautiful thing about gratitude is that it always comes back around and creates something even more beautiful than how it started.

The business needs to show appreciation and give gratitude to both the leaders who are being highlighted in the stories and the people who are capturing the stories; the people capturing the stories are leaders in their own right. **Make it mean something** is about saying *thank you* in a way that's genuine, authentic, and filled with compassion. When the leadership proof point concept is done right, when you start making contributions mean something, people will start contributing stories and showing up with compassion in unique ways just because they want to feel gratitude.

The Attitude Bar: Serving Kool-Aid, Coffee, and Cocktails

Innovation does not happen just because a business decides to create a colorful or contemporary room, or sends leaders to a workshop where they learn the latest innovation techniques. Sam learned that lesson the hard way when the team found themselves still struggling after completing the three-year strategy. It's only when the business builds trust, demonstrates compassion, and gives freedom that a business has circulated enough healthy energy that it can become innovative. You see, trust, compassion, and freedom create the magic pill for innovation. That magic pill is called attitude.

Freedom turns ideas and vision into reality, because freedom is the final component in creating an attitude that *anything is possible*, and innovation comes from that attitude. Attitude is how progress is born. When the business has circulated enough healthy energy to create the attitude that anything is possible, you'll know it. It's then that culture is at its best, people are engaged, and the internal brand becomes so strong that everyone can't help but drink the Kool-Aid, coffee, or cocktails you're serving. When the internal brand is the attitude that anything is possible, everyone becomes engaged because the healthy energy feels too good not to be part of the journey.

Chapter Highlights

* **Freedom turns ideas and vision into reality.** True freedom is only possible when trust and compassion are present. There's no other way.

* The heart chakra of your businesses must be clear, balanced, and circulating healthy energy if you have any desire for innovation. If it's not clear, turning ideas and vision into reality become increasingly more difficult.

✳ Trust is being able to express yourself freely, openly, and without hesitation because you feel protected and safe from having to experience shame, physical harm, hurt, or guilt.

✳ We all have a trust curve, and we put everyone we know somewhere on it. That also means that you're on someone else's trust curve.

✳ You can't have trust without compassion. It's a guarantee that if someone doesn't see you as a compassionate human being, you are not high on her personal trust curve.

✳ Freedom is the final component in creating an attitude that *anything is possible*, and innovation comes from that attitude. Attitude is how progress is born.

✳ When the internal brand is the attitude that *anything is possible*, everyone becomes engaged because the healthy energy feels too good not to be part of the journey.

✳ Leveraging the Trust Curve Assessment and Proof Point Leadership concept is how your business can begin living Business Principle #5.

Principle #6
Creative Expression Fuels Change and Growth

Principle #5 was all about the trust, compassion, and freedom you give to other people, the outward actions that create an *anything is possible* attitude. Principle #6 is about the trust, compassion, and freedom you give *yourself*, internal actions that fuel creative expression. In order for both principles to exist, and effectively support a healthy energy ecosystem, everyone needs to feel worthy of receiving trust, compassion, and freedom, from both themselves and others in the business.

It's often easier for us to receive good energy from other people than it is to receive good energy from ourselves. As difficult as it is, individually, every person in your business needs to pay attention to the trust, compassion, and freedom he gives himself, because it's the trust, compassion, and freedom we give ourselves that makes us feel worthy and deserving of healthy energy. The challenge is that people are only willing to give and receive these things from themselves when they have a strong sense of self—self-confidence, self-empowerment, and self-respect. For this reason, Principle #6 gets personal and addresses the "self" of every person in your business.

In a human, the solar plexus chakra is the home of *self*. It's located right above the navel and below the heart. When the solar plexus is off balance, you're flooded with anxiety driven by fear of the unknown. You worry about what other people are thinking about you, how other people are judging you, if you are disappointing those around you, whether you're living up to the standards of all the external influences in your life—even if those standards are unhealthy and toxic to you as a human being. When your solar plexus is off balance, you give away your "self" in order to appease judgments being made by everyone and everything else in your life except you, and you struggle with receiving positive energy.

The solar plexus chakra of your business is no different, because it's directly related to the solar plexus of each individual person in your business—the collective body. It's the intersection between what's going on inside the minds of every person in the business and the business itself. This intersection, where the energetic health of your business is most visible, is called *culture*. If you have a collective body of people who lack self-confidence, self-empowerment, and self-respect you have a dysfunctional culture that will not circulate healthy energy or profits without a fight. Balancing the solar plexus of your business is possible, but it requires you to have a genuine interest in providing personal development to each individual who is part of the business. The business needs to help people remember they have personal power, have the right to create personal boundaries, and are deserving of holding an attitude that anything is possible. It's only then that people will give themselves trust, compassion, and freedom to show up authentically. And only then will people creatively express themselves in a way that will fuel change and growth for your business.

Personal Power

Do you ever wake up in the morning with a feeling of anxiety in the pit of your stomach? Having no idea what the day has in store for you, but convinced that "thing" that's giving you the churning stomach is no doubt going to continue causing havoc in your life? The anxiety is almost unbearable, and it causes you to doubt some or all aspects of yourself. All you can do is muster up just enough energy to get ready and head out the door to face "it"—or at least survive. This is what life feels like when you've given away your personal power and when you're living your life to satisfy everyone but yourself.

The solar plexus is the most difficult chakra to balance and keep healthy, because it's the intersection of our self and the rest of the world. The emotions we experience within our solar plexus represent whether we are showing up to the world honoring ourselves or giving away our personal power on a silver platter. Our solar plexus is not shy, and it's all about tough love. The minute you're not honoring yourself, respecting yourself, or having confidence in yourself, your solar plexus will become flooded with emotions of anxiety, self-doubt, fear of the unknown, chaos, shame, guilt, hurt, and self-denigration—emotions that are screaming, "Wake up! You are worthy of self-respect, self-confidence, and self-empowerment. Stop giving it way." You might be thinking, *I have plenty of self-confidence, self-respect, and self-empowerment going on, thank you.* And you might. That's fantastic. You can be a mentor for everyone in your business who struggles with the idea of "self." However, before you get too excited, think about the following.

Think about that one person in your life for whom you have the most respect. Maybe this is a person you know, or maybe it's someone you don't know but admire greatly. This is a person to whom you would never say no unless absolutely necessary, and for great reason. This is a person you would do anything for, stop anything for, and defend if ever needed. Who is this person? Think long and hard.

Now here's the reality: If this person you're thinking about isn't yourself, you're giving away your personal power to everyone and everything else in your life instead of using it for what it's meant for—you. The only way you're going to eliminate the anxiety in the pit of your stomach is if you start taking back what was always yours to begin with—your personal power.

I learned to love my solar plexus the hard way. I didn't just wake up one morning automatically self-confident, feeling a sense of personal power, and honoring myself. Nope. My solar plexus and I had a long, drawn-out, bloody fight for years. And it wasn't until the last few years that I allowed my solar plexus to win. You see, I'm no different from every person working in your business: I grew up chasing external approval, found myself getting false power from material accomplishments, and strategically aligned my next steps based on the judgments of people around me. Setting out to prove to the world that I mattered, I found myself filled with anxiety every day because I was constantly living in the future, while carrying fear that I wasn't living up to the standards other people had of me in the present. I couldn't get out of my head. I was tired and felt beat up. With all the personal and work chaos that seemed to be a constant flow in my life, all I wanted to do was stop for one minute and experience what it was like to just *be*. That's what all the Zen people in my life kept telling me. "You just have to learn how to *be* and put yourself first." I remember thinking, *What the hell does that mean? I take care of myself just fine. How do these Zen people stay present?* I even bought books, became an aspiring yogi, and started running in an effort to learn how to be present. It didn't work.

So instead of continuing to try and figure it out, I decided denial was the best alternative. I was so good at denial that I figured out how to label my inability to be present, as well as my choice of giving away all my personal power, as my strength. Yep. I called it "being futuristic" and "being an achiever." You can imagine how excited I was when Marcus Buckingham and Donald O. Clifton's book *Now, Discover Your Strengths* came out in 2001 and proved I was right: Being futuristic and being an achiever are both strengths! You see, I just decided to ignore the first part of the book that talks about how your strengths can actually be your worst enemy until you learn how to productively turn them into strengths. I thought, *Small points. I'm already so good at this futuristic achiever thing, I don't need to worry about that part of the book.* Meanwhile, I was still in the trap, and kept giving all my personal power to everyone else on a silver platter, while having no idea what was really going on around me, because I was actually living completely in the future—choosing to live with anxiety, stress, and exhaustion. Some people have the opposite problem: They live in the past. Both are energetically unhealthy, and both will destroy self-confidence and self-worth in a heartbeat.

So here's what keeping your personal power looks like, and why being present is so important. If you're not doing any of these practices you're giving away your power on a silver platter, and you're choosing to swim in a pool of toxic energy. If you have a business that involves people, there's a good chance every person in the business, regardless of title, is also giving away some (if not all) of their personal power. The goal of an energetically healthy business is to support everyone in their quest to actively live the following seven practices:

1. Own only what is yours.

2. Honor your values.

3. Forgive yourself and others.

4. State what you want.

5. Let it go, and move on.

6. If it doesn't fit, don't buy it.

7. Accept nothing other than respect—period.

Own Only What Is Yours

Most people go through the day packing luggage for a trip they don't even want to go on. This luggage quickly becomes baggage filled with unhealthy energy. Here's an example of the type of baggage we put into our luggage throughout the day.

Let's say you have made an apology, because you chose to take responsibility for something you did or didn't do. The person you made the apology to never even acknowledged it was made. Instead of letting it go, you pack anxiety, hurt, disappointment, and even fear into your luggage. Even though you owned your part, the fact that they still have emotions tied to the situation makes you still want to hang on. Here's the deal: Their emotions are not yours. Let it go. Move on. If they don't want to acknowledge the fact that you took responsibility for your actions, the rest is not yours to carry. Feel good about the fact that you owned what was yours, and move on. This is true for any emotion, in any type of relationship. If it's not yours, don't own it. Take a good solid look at the baggage you're carrying and unpack everything that's not yours. If you're thinking, *It's not that easy*, you're right. No one said it was going to be easy. However making the choice to *not* own it is the hardest part. The rest is taken care of by time.

Honor Your Values

Principle #4 was all about your purpose and identifying your values. Personal power is all about honoring them. If something in your life or the business doesn't align with your values, then you need to make the change that moves you into alignment. Until you do, there's no one in this world you can blame for the situation you're in except yourself. Here's the beautiful thing: Oftentimes the change needed is simply of mindset. Sometimes, yes, significant action is needed, but many times it's a mindset switch. Having personal power means that, in your mind, you see yourself as the most important person in your life. Until you choose to honor yourself and your values through both thought and action, you will continue to give away the power that's rightfully yours. When you put yourself first by honoring your values, your healthy energy is magnified throughout the business and throughout your life. Everything in your presence benefits and becomes better.

Forgive Yourself and Others

So many people in this world give away their personal power because they choose to hold on to grudges. They disparage themselves for past choices, and punish themselves by not forgiving themselves. They refuse to forgive other people because they don't believe other people deserve their forgiveness. This is called the blame game, and it's a game that no one will ever win.

What most people don't understand is that when you choose not to forgive, you're choosing to covet negative energy that's harming every aspect of your life. Every time you choose to hang on to something that simply needs to be let go of and forgiven, you're choosing to live your life swimming in a pool of negative energy. It's your choice. It always is. However, you will never attain a life or a business of healthy energy if you refuse to forgive. There's no way around this one. You can try, but the result is always the same: A lack of forgiveness fills up your baggage like a ton of bricks. Again, it's a mindset. Sometimes forgiveness requires actions, but most of the time, it's about making the choice to forgive and let go. Remember, forgiveness is always more about you than the other person.

State What You Want

Being able to state what you want is the essence of personal power. It's not enough to identify and live your values; you need to look at your life and literally state what you want within every aspect of your existence. That includes everything from the intricacies of a work project to big life aspirations. It doesn't matter the size of the *want*; unless you state it, there's no guarantee you'll get it. The first part of stating what you want is stating it to yourself. The second part is stating what you want to the rest of the world—clearly and with respect.

Not taking the time to state what you want can often turn into passive-aggressive behavior, a technique that is guaranteed to derail your personal power and relationships. It doesn't matter if you're Minnesota Nice or a Georgia Peach, if you use passive-aggressive behavior to manipulate someone else to get what you want, instead of stating what you want outright, you're being hurtful and will be perceived as manipulative. If you choose to be passive aggressive, people will resent you, won't want to be around you, and won't trust you, because they will always feel that you have an ulterior motive that doesn't have their best interests in mind. Being passive aggressive is a form of dysfunctional behavior.

When people haven't taken the time to really figure out what they want and name it, they react to situations and interactions on emotion alone. If the situation or interaction is not generating feel-good emotions, people resort to guilt, shame, and hurtful techniques out of self-protection, in order to feel valued and respected. You see, most of the time, passive-aggressive behavior comes from people who lack personal power; they desperately want to be heard, yet have no idea how to use their voice to state what they want. To reclaim your personal power, you need to figure out what you want, name it, and take responsibility for getting what you want in a healthy way.

Let it Go, and Move On

This is the most significant challenge people have when it comes to keeping their personal power. You'll notice that *letting it go, and moving on* comes up in every personal power practice—it's the red thread that unites all the practices together. And it takes practice, conscious effort, and deliberate intention to make it happen. Let me be clear: Letting it go and moving on does not mean that you condone behavior that is wrong. It means that you don't own the poor choices and negative emotions other people are choosing to put into this world. Yes, state your piece respectfully. Make it clear that you own what is yours. Be intentional about having the other person's best interests in mind. Take responsibility for your own emotions and choices. And when you're in the wrong, admit it and apologize—no matter how hard that may be. However, once you name it, and take responsibility for your own actions in a healthy way, let it go and move on. Life is much sweeter, and feels that much easier when you're not carrying other people's baggage.

If It Doesn't Fit, Don't Buy It

In business, we love to give and receive feedback. We say things like, "Here are your areas of opportunity. I see your challenge as being...." Sure, sometimes the feedback is spot-on, and you should be thankful someone actually shared her opinion with you. Sometimes it's not. If it doesn't fit, don't buy it. Guess what? You have that right. It doesn't matter how high up the chain of command the person who has given you the feedback is, if it doesn't fit, you have the right not to buy it.

I had a client of mine come to me absolutely distraught after receiving her annual review. She was distraught because her leader gave her feedback that she felt was inaccurate. In fact, she even had proof that the feedback was wrong. My response was this: "You have a choice. You can choose to accept it, or you can choose not to buy it. If you choose not to buy it, you have to forgive them for giving inaccurate information, and then you need to let it go and move on. If you choose not to forgive them, you can't move on. Are you going to buy it, or are you going to forgive and move on?" She chose to forgive and move on—and she did a damn good job of it.

Accept Nothing Other Than Respect—Period

You, along with every person in your business, are a human being who deserves respect and is worthy of personal power. No matter a person's title, age, generation, skin color, gender, or belief system, no one deserves anything other than genuine, authentic respect. Most people will logically understand and believe this in concept, but even today the action of disrespect is everywhere in business. We still treat people like cogs. Dysfunctional leaders still think it's okay to treat other people who have less of a title as less important. Discrimination is still everywhere. We can all pretend that the issues of yesterday are no longer the issues of today, but that's not the case. And until every human being shows up in your business treating every other human being in your business with respect, toxic energetic cancer will continue to spread throughout your business.

Accepting nothing other than respect is a two-way street—and you need to own both sides of the street. That means that you show up each day and choose to see other people as human beings who hurt, love, laugh, and are trying to make it through this world just like you. It also means that in those moments when you're being disrespected, you meet those moments with respect by choosing to see that person as a human being who hurts, loves, laughs, and is trying to make it through this world just like you. It means that in those moments of adversity, you respectfully state your piece, stand up for yourself, take responsibility by owning what's yours, and remove yourself whenever necessary, but then you forgive, let go, and move on. Accepting nothing other than respect is just that—regardless the side of the street you're standing on, you need to require respect to be given by both you and the other party. Disrespect is never okay, and the only way we're going to change this world, the only way you're going to reclaim your personal power, is to make respect a non-negotiable for how you live your life.

✳✳✳

Here's how I finally figured out how to stay present. It wasn't through all the books I read, my aspirations to be a yogi, or all the running I did—though those things were beneficial to my mind and body. I felt great physically, but I still wasn't present. I was still swimming in the pool of harmful energy and anxiety—just giving away my personal power. Then one evening it hit me. I was driving around my neighborhood, listening to music, and signing very loudly; it's one of my favorite things to do at the end of the day. All of a sudden, I pulled over, stopped the car, and just stared. I stared because everything looked different. I remember looking at the trees and thinking, *Oh my God, they look like completely different trees. They're beautiful.* So I started the car again and kept driving. Cynical, I wanted to see if this amazing feeling was going to go away. It didn't. All the way home, everything looked different. When I got home, I gasped in shock. I realized that I had driven all the way home thinking about nothing except the trees—nothing at all but the trees. There wasn't a single thought that crossed my mind except the trees. It was amazing. And in that moment I realized it was the first time I was present.

I've thought about that moment a lot, because that moment happens now repeatedly. I actually have to intentionally try to remember what it was it like when I wasn't ever present—and it's hard to remember. I now know how I got here. It wasn't easy. It took a few people in my life to shake sense into me, and quite a few experiences that forced me outside my comfort zone. And chip by chip I took my brick wall of self-protection down until it didn't exist anymore. Now I stand completely vulnerable to the world and I'm not scared—because I get it. I took back my personal power. I own only what is mine. I honor my values. I forgive myself, and others, unconditionally. I state what I want. I let it go, and move on. I only buy what fits. And I accept nothing other than respect—period.

My best friend, the greatest healer of our time, taught me a little statement that works wonders in my life. Anytime I feel slimed with toxic energy that's not mine, I say this statement out loud, and it reminds me that I have choice in this world, and I choose not to own anyone's emotions and actions but my own. That little statement is this: "What's theirs is theirs. What's mine is mine. Let none of theirs be mine. And let none of mine be theirs."

I continue to be amazed by how words create energy that protect us from harmful energetic toxicity that others are choosing to put into this world. Go ahead, try the statement out yourself; it's amazing. It's important to realize that the statement is not meant to "fix" the other person. It just allows you to walk away without any of their energetic green slime all over you. It's the reminder that you have a choice to walk away clean, and with all your personal power intact. What they choose to do is not yours to carry. Let it go, and move on.

There's a Chinese proverb that rings true in my life, and it's a great litmus test that keeps me in check. As do most people, I still have moments when I feel depressed or filled with anxiety. That's just life. However, those moments are now just that—moments. And I now understand how to name why those moments are happening so I can move on. Here's the proverb:

"If you are depressed, you are living in the past. If you are anxious, you are living in the future. If you are at peace, you are living in the present."

—Lao Tsu

Boundaries

We can't talk about self-confidence, self-empowerment, and self-respect without talking about boundaries. Boundaries are intentional acts of separation between you and another person whom you believe is not treating you with kindness, respect, and a sense of humanity. Boundaries say, "If you choose to treat me with disrespect and hurtful, guilt-ridden techniques, you are not allowed to be part of my world. I am self-confident and self-empowered, and have self-respect. And I choose to only surround myself with those people who understand, support, and respect me—period. Treating me with kindness, respect, and a sense of humanity is not optional." Boundaries are necessary when you need to keep yourself healthy and free from toxic energy others are choosing to put into the world.

It's very difficult to maintain a sense of self-confidence, self-empowerment, and self-respect when you have people around you who don't respect your energy. If they're not respecting your energy, they're not respecting you, and you need to create a boundary. To create boundaries you have to name these people, and consciously make a decision to only associate with them when necessary. Yes, you're going to name people in the business whom you see and work with every day. That's okay. See them and work with them, but know you have intentionally created a boundary that states their energy, their emotions, and their choices are theirs and not yours. And make a commitment to yourself that until this person can show up in life as a healthy, functional human being, your interactions will only be out of necessity. Remember, "What's theirs is theirs. What's mine is mine. Let none of theirs be mine. And let none of mine be theirs." Here's the beauty about boundaries: Everyone thinks you have to state out loud to a specific person that you have created a boundary and they're on the other side of it, but, through the power of energy and intention, simply stating to yourself that you've created a boundary will make that boundary appear.

In a business that thrives on healthy energy, boundaries are less of an issue, because once a business is able to circulate healthy energy throughout its culture, respect is everywhere and the need for boundaries lessens. Notice I said *lessens*, not *dissipates*. No matter how good the energy in your business is, you will always have people in different phases of owning their personal power. You will most likely never have a business where everyone is 100-percent self-confident, self-empowered, and full of self-respect. It's a process, and the journey is different for everyone.

The last piece on boundaries is the most important, and it goes back to the personal power practice of accepting nothing less than respect: Never create a boundary out of anger, hurt, shame, or guilt. The minute you do, all that negative energy ends up getting stuck on your side of the boundary, and it becomes incredibly difficult to get rid of. A boundary made from anger, hurt, shame, and guilt is a boundary rooted in baggage that you now get to carry with you everywhere—even though it's not yours to carry. Before you set a boundary, make sure you can see the other person as a human being who hurts, loves, laughs, and is trying to make it through this world just as you are. Set the boundary with his best interests in mind, and with the intention that the boundary won't have to last forever. Boundaries are purposefully meant to give people the space and time they need to establish strength in self-confidence, self-empowerment, and self-respect. That strength will resurface through amazing creative expression that will no doubt fuel change and growth for your business.

Energy Vampires

Reclaiming your personal power and learning how to set boundaries is a process. As you're venturing into the process it's important that you know a type of person called the *energy vampire*. Heard of them? These are the people who suck your energy dry because they don't completely understand how to respect energetic boundaries. Remember the example in the Introduction of how there are people in this world who, when walking your way, make you literally want to run for the hills? These people may be wonderful, and you may actually like them in theory, but their energy makes you want to run. They enter your office for a quick chat, and the minute they leave, you feel as though you've just been put through the ringer and energetically slimed by their mere presence. Ugh. In fact, the minute you sense this person coming toward you, you get an overwhelming feeling of "Oh God, I need to get the hell out of here!" You know those people.

Here's the deal: Businesses of every size have energy vampires. I know you don't want to hear this, but you yourself are at times the vampire. Yes, there are times you haven't respected boundaries and have sucked other people's energy dry. Don't worry, you're most likely not doing this consciously. That being said, energy vampires are everywhere. The vampire syndrome is on the rise. We're in a human energy crisis, and people are desperate for healthy energy regardless of how they get it. And until everyone in your business understands the concept of energy vampires, and is able to create healthy boundaries and reclaim their person power, these vampires will continue to clog your business's energy system with energetic disease. Here are a few examples of how energy vampires show up in business.

✳ ***The Victim:*** The Victim constantly shows up to share with you every detail about how he has been "wronged." The Victim, of course, is *never* responsible for any problems he has experienced. And, in a very clever way, the Victim is somehow able to squeeze in his statements of victimhood during every conversation you have, no matter how short. In the meantime, he just happens to suck your energy for an added boost to his energy. He always feels so much better after talking to you, and you always feel completely drained.

* ***The Cynic:*** The Cynic is *not* the colleague who's great at playing the devil's advocate, though this can be a gray area if you're not careful. The Cynic shows up to shower everyone with negativity as a means to share with the rest of the world how dark her part of the world feels. Oftentimes, the Cynic is going through troublesome times personally. A dark cloud seems to be following her throughout the day, and she chooses, consciously or not, to rain on the parade of anyone with different ideas and perspectives as a means to shed her feelings of internal bewilderment. At the end of the conversation, the Cynic feels better because she added "value" to the team, while the rest of the team feels exhausted.
* ***The Power Monger:*** You're in a good mood and the Power Monger sucks your energy just because he can. And you let him. Sometimes this person has perceived power over you, such as a title, and sometime this person is a part-time Joe who just shows up in your office. This may be the person who always seems pleasant. In fact, after every conversation you have with him, you can't figure out why you're so exhausted. What has happened is he has energetically hooked into your energy and taken it. Little too "New Age" for you? Ask yourself why you're so drained the next time "Mary Poppins" swings by.

Regardless of how energy vampires show up at your business, the remedy is awareness and setting boundaries. Consciously make the choice to not take other people's good energy for your own personal use; it's disrespectful. A great first step in reviving the energy in your business is to share this information with everyone. I guarantee you'll feel a positive difference. Test it. Once people understand what an energy vampire is, no one will want to be one.

Environment

An *anything is possible* attitude needs to show up in the look and feel of the business environment. Your business environment is just as important for creative expression as are personal power and boundaries. If you want people to creatively express themselves and be able to fuel change and growth for your business, and you want to circulate healthy energy throughout your business, you need a visible environment that communicates trust, compassion, and freedom.

Having a C-suite in mahogany row and everyone else in gray cubicle land is *not* going to work. Let me be clear: I love mahogany; it's beautiful. In fact, if you want everyone in the business to have mahogany, go for it; make it happen. The problem is not mahogany. The problem is if your business is creating luxury for people at the top while everyone else gets leftovers. It communicates to the rest of the business that everyone else is a second-class citizen, who doesn't deserve the same respect as the people sitting in mahogany row. If this sounds like your business, you need to change it if you are to have any hope of creating an energy ecosystem that circulates healthy energy. If you choose to visibly separate and create different classes of people, you are choosing an environment that sucks human energy, inspiration, creative expression, and an *anything is possible* attitude dry. You are choosing toxic energy. If your environment makes a statement of "You are not worthy, because you are *less than* the people at the top," people will *never* feel safe to creatively express themselves in the way your business needs them to in order to move forward in the future.

I've read many success stories of businesses that have proven that equalizing the business environment fuels creative expression. Google is just one example of a large business that has proven that an equal and open environment works. Google also has a "Don't be Evil" philosophy that permeates the business and fuels people with a sense of freedom. The environment, together with their "Don't be evil" philosophy, creates trust. People feel genuinely safe to express themselves in a way that moves the business forward. Google is huge; what happens if your business is small? Another example is Network Medics, a small technology firm based in the Twin Cities, managed by three owners who decided to give *everyone* an office. Not only does everyone have an office, but everyone chooses the exact furniture and design they want. Everyone's office looks completely different, and everyone's office matches his or her own personality. It's amazing; you can feel the energy of trust, compassion, and freedom as soon as you walk through the doors. Everyone at Network Medics genuinely feels safe to creatively expressive themselves in a way that moves the business forward. The business, each client, and every person in the business benefits. Both Google and Network Medics have chosen to circulate healthy energy.

The importance of environment goes beyond people's "workstations." In order to have an energy ecosystem that circulates healthy energy, people need to be able to breathe—literally! Your business needs plants, natural light, and color. You might even want to throw in a fish here and there; fish give off good energy. Let people open their windows—they're not going to jump. People thrive on nature, light, and color. People thrive when they're in an open environment that is authentically equal. Gray and beige cubicles flanked by mahogany row will not foster creativity, and people will not feel safe to express themselves in the way your business needs them to. Take a note from Google and Network Medics and create an equally open environment that fuels change and growth.

Designers always ask the same question before jumping in and redesigning your home or office. The question is simple, but is often difficult to answer: "What do you want?" After they get a blank look, they ask the follow-up question, "What words describe the feeling you want your home or office to have?" Seriously, it's always those two questions. When it comes to an energetically healthy business, the answer is always the same.

If you want an energetically healthy environment that energizes people, ignites action, and drives sustainable profit, here's your response. "I want an environment that conveys trust, compassion, and freedom. I want people to walk in and immediately feel as though anything is possible. People should walk through every part of the business feeling able to breath, and feeling as though they are worthy of being part of a business that genuinely cares about their well-being. I want every aspect of the environment to support every person in giving themselves trust, compassion, and freedom, so they can creatively express themselves in a way that fuels change and growth for the business." The process is simple. Make it happen.

The Process: Micro Communities

To balance the solar plexus chakra of your business, you need to help people remember they have personal power and the right to create personal boundaries, and you need to create an environment that communicates the message that all people are worthy of holding an attitude that anything is possible. Once you accomplish those three things, people will give themselves freedom to show up authentically; only then will creative expression fuel change and growth for your business. Until this is accomplished, people will remain resistant to change and will lack the desire to move any new ideas forward. Here's how you do it.

Contrary to the title *Personal Power*, reclaiming personal power does not happen solo. In fact, the people who are most successful in reclaiming their personal power and living the seven practices have done so because they were surrounded by a small community of people who cared enough to help them along the way. Your business has to create these Micro Communities that allow people to practice their power, name their boundaries, and build confidence before they will be willing to make themselves vulnerable to the rest of the world.

Micro Communities are small groups of people who come together on a weekly basis to support and encourage each other's progress. This concept is not new. In fact, the idea of "support groups" or "small groups" has been recognized for years, in different capacities around the world. They're recognized globally because they work: People succeed at higher levels when they feel supported by other people. Your business is no different. We are all humans, with very human lives that are difficult and taxing. We all need support and reminders to keep hold of our personal power, create boundaries, and to be intentional about putting healthy energy into the world. It's incredibly difficult to succeed at those three elements by yourself.

Here's how you build Micro Communities throughout your business and what the experience looks like.

* Micro Communities should consist of no more than seven people and no less than four. Ideally, each community is made up of five people.

* Micro Communities meet once a week. (No, once a month is not enough.)

* Micro Communities need to be made a priority for the business. The minute they are seen as an extracurricular "fun committee" activity, they will not work. If that's your mindset, you need to re-read Principle #1: Functional leaders drive profits. Micro Communities need to be set up as part of standard operation, not as an extra engagement effort.

* The business has the responsibility for giving permission for Micro Communities to exist.

* Leaders cannot give people a hard time for being part of a Micro Community.

* Every leader needs to be part of a Micro Community.

* Groups are put together through a lottery system, with the only caveat being geography: It's best to keep telecommuters

together, and organize non-telecommuter communities with people who can see each other face to face if at all possible.

✳ A dedicated online portal for each Micro Community is helpful, but not necessary.

Each week Micro Communities come together and ask themselves how the seven practices of reclaiming personal power showed up in the previous week for each of them. Some people will have a great deal to share; others won't. Some people will assume the role of a coach, and some will simply observe and just be present. There are no rules, other than respect and confidentiality. The agenda is simple: ***How did the following practices of personal power show up this week? What did you do? Were boundaries necessary? How does this change how will you show up next week?***

1. Own only what is yours.

2. Honor your values.

3. Forgive yourself and others.

4. State what you want.

5. Let it go, and move on.

6. If it doesn't fit, don't buy it.

7. Accept nothing other than respect—period.

Micro Communities can be successful no matter how diverse or counterintuitive: co-ed, telecommuter-only, or made up of people with vastly different titles and levels of responsibility for the business. The outcome is always the same: People in each Micro Community build strong friendships, successfully start reclaiming their personal power, and learn how to establish boundaries. The business benefits from the fact that people start enjoying their work because they feel part of something greater than themselves. The result is healthy energy, and the solar plexus of your business begins to balance.

Chapter Highlights

✳ **Creative expression fuels change and growth.**

✳ Change and growth are propelled forward by environment.
A healthy visual and cultural environment breeds confidence
in individuality, intellect, and common sense. Sitting at the
solar plexus chakra of the business, it's environment that
gives people permission, protection, and freedom to move
the business forward.

✳ Until everyone in the business feels personally *worthy* and
deserving of having an *anything is possible* attitude, creative
expression and innovation will remain the latest buzzwords
that seem unattainable, costly, and absolutely exhausting. To
balance the solar plexus of the business, the business simply
needs to help people remember they have personal power
and the right to create personal boundaries, and are worthy
of holding an attitude that anything is possible.

✳ Everyone in the business needs to reclaim their personal
power by living seven critical practices:

  1. Own only what is yours.

  2. Honor your values.

  3. Forgive yourself and others.

  4. State what you want.

  5. Let it go, and move on.

  6. If it doesn't fit, don't buy it.

  7. Accept nothing other than respect—period.

✳ Stay present, and create boundaries when necessary. Never
create a boundary out of anger, hurt, shame, or guilt. The
minute you do, all that negative energy ends up getting
stuck on your side of the boundary, and it becomes
incredibly difficult to get rid of.

✳ An *anything is possible* attitude needs to show up in the look and feel of the business environment. Your business environment is just as important to creative expression as personal power and boundaries.

✳ Micro Communities allow people to practice their power, name their boundaries, and build confidence before they are willing to make themselves vulnerable to the rest of the business.

Principle #7

Human Connectivity Is the Source of Energy

This chapter is all about human connectivity, and how human connection drives profit. Principle #7 sits at the sacral chakra of your business, the energy center that's all about emotion and relationships. Principle #7 reminds us that we are all one and interconnected through energy, and because we're connected, we feel what's going on around us, and the result is either inspiration or depletion. Putting people first, one-on-one relationships, leadership transparency, and diversity efforts fuel this energy center. When the sacral chakra of your business is balanced people feel valued, accept change easily, and are motivated to act in ways that drive profit.

We are born to connect. Regardless of belief or spiritual understanding, one commonality exists among every human being on
this planet. We are born to connect. We walk through this life in
synchrony with every other human being in this world. Whether
ordering coffee at the local coffee shop, driving down the road solo,
being around close friends and family, or watching television at the
end of the day, we are connecting with other people every day in
some way, shape, or form. You might be thinking, *I'm not with anyone when I'm in my car. And I watch television to get away from people
and relax from the intensity of my day. There's no one but me in those
scenarios.* True, you are alone. However, when you're driving, you
are (or at least should be) conscious of other drivers on the road, and
how your driving impacts them—and you're not typically alone on
the road. When you're watching TV, you're watching people, even if
those people are animated or shown as creatures from other worlds.
You're connecting with the beings you're watching, and people created that television show to connect with you.

The importance of human connection is a critical concept for
you to understand if you want your business to be fueled with
healthy energy and if you want to drive profits functionally. People
get energy from other people. Feeling valued and genuinely accepted for who and what we are as human beings fuels us. By nature, we
look to the interactions we have with other people to help validate
whether we are valued and accepted. This is called a meaningful
connection, and as a society, we are starved for meaningful connec-
tions. This starvation is causing the human energy crisis, and the
crisis is fueled not because of our busy schedules, but because our
schedules and the way our world operates today are limiting our energy source: healthy human connection, physical connection with
other people that makes us feel valued and accepted.

Principle #4 and #6 were necessary to learn first because they
teach us how to value and accept ourselves, and they prepare us for
the most critical success factor in business: Principle #7, the ability for everyone to authentically connect with other human beings

in a way that says, "You are valued and accepted." It's only then that anyone can truly give and receive healthy energy. People in your business have to hear, see, and feel that they are valued and accepted for who and what they are. There's not a human being on Earth who doesn't want to feel valued and accepted by the rest of humanity. It's in those moments when people feel valued and accepted that they become filled with healthy energy and everything in your business benefits. The following story is an example of what happens when a business consciously or unconsciously strips away opportunities for people to hear, see, and feel that they are valued and accepted for who and what they are.

Steve is an owner of a medical device business. The business has experienced great success in the past 20 years. It has doubled in size in the past 10 years, and in the past five years it has embarked on a huge change effort. The intent of the change effort was to restructure its operation to be more accommodating to the people involved with the business and also to make more profit. The change effort included opening two more remote offices located in California and Ohio. Currently, the company has more than 20 remote offices, 750 people working across the nation, and 50 percent of the workforce population is telecommuters. In fact, one of the benefits of working for the company is the freedom people have to work during the hours when they're most productive. Steve calls this Smart Hard Work, or SHW. He realized that the company could double its efficiencies and increase profits by allowing people to manage their own schedules in their own way—a results-based work environment.

As part of the results-based work environment, Steve made sure everyone in the business had a smart phone, laptop, and tablet, and each office facility has 24-hour access for people to come and go as they please. Each location across the nation has an open environment design that promotes freedom and creativity. From sales to operations, every person and every leader has the autonomy to organize and manage their team and work in a way that will best meet the needs of the business. There are, of course, processes throughout the business that are necessary for the production and quality of products and services to the client, but people are trusted to follow the process, and are measured on the results they and their team produce. Everything in the business is set up on cloud computing, and the business model is fueled on private labeling—there's absolutely no need for costly manufacturing facilities. From the outside, the business appears to be the ideal work environment and business model, and profits throughout the years proved the assumption accurate.

Everyone in the business worked extremely hard to create this ideal business environment that would, in theory, maintain high engagement, retention, and loyalty levels, along with increasing profitability. The change effort took almost three years to complete, the two new locations being the final elements of the project. Workdays across the company were filled with people working together on special projects. Even teams that were remote came together in person more often to get the plan done. People were thrilled that the project was coming to an end, but never once complained about the extra time and effort they were putting into the business. During the change effort people developed strong relationships, became friends, and were highly engaged and loyal to the business. In fact, during the change effort, people across the business were actually referring friends to become part of the team because it was fun place to work and everyone was optimistic about the future.

With the exception of the last two locations, where only a few people are working, the change project came to a completion a year and a half ago. Recently, Steve noticed a few concerning declines in key performance indicators for the business. Engagement scores started to decline, and for the first time in years, retention started to become an issue; people didn't seem nearly as enthused to be part of the business as they did a few years back. In fact, the retention numbers during the last six months indicated that people didn't have the loyalty they once had to the business. Sure, the struggles in the economy put more stress on people, and the change was hard, but the business had experienced those phases in years past and always seemed to recover easily. Something was different this time. People seemed more tired than usual, even though the project was done and for the most part everyone has settled back into business-as-usual activity. Steve was concerned. The new business model, the autonomy being given across the company, and taking everything virtual was suppose to improve already great results.

Steve and his executive team weren't quite sure what was going on or what they could do differently. The new business model was textbook and incorporated everything the experts and case studies showed worked. Every part of the business was solid. Processes were in place, and products and services responded to market needs. The team even hired a high-end outside consulting firm to validate the accuracy of the business structure and to help manage the change process. Sales of products and services continued moving forward as projected, but the internal operation, and the service clients received after the initial sale, started to become troubling. Clients even started to move to their competitors—another significant red flag that something was wrong and needed to be fixed.

Steve's business is suffering from what most businesses are suffering from today: the human energy crisis. Steve's business is an example of how you can do everything according to what the latest management books say, and still be impacted by the lack of energy people are experiencing. The problem was that the new business model actually stripped away the very thing that fuels a business with healthy energy: real human connection. People had spent three years hearing, seeing, and feeling the energy from one another, and then it was gone. People need to connect to each other, and if they're not connecting to each other in your business, they will find other ways outside your business to experience the connection. Energetically healthy businesses figure out how to create points of human connection throughout the operation, so people will choose to stay and seek out what they need to exist as a human being in the business environment in which they work.

So the solution to Steve's challenge concerning engagement, retention, and loyalty is to add human connectivity back into the business model. You see, the reason why Steve's business was experiencing a decline in engagement, and struggling with retention and loyalty, was that the business was lacking energy nutrients: real human connection. The new business model was great, but it stripped away the energetic nutrients people desperately need in order to stay engaged and loyal. People in Steve's company became disengaged after the change effort was complete, not because the business model wasn't ideal, but because they no longer had the human interaction within the business that made them feel valued and accepted as human beings. The business needs to make creating and maintaining strong relationships with one another an even greater priority than cloud computing and flexible operating standards. Again, the new business model is great, but now Steve needs to figure out how to incorporate authentic human connection back into the business so the business itself doesn't lose its soul.

Energy Nutrients

Intentionally adding functional human connection to your business model is critically important. Energy is like food for the body: If you eat food that is filled with empty calories and lacks nutrients, your body will respond with physical pain, obesity, and a greater feeling of hunger. Your body needs vitamins, minerals, and real nutrients to survive and feel good. Rich, nutrient-based food can only come from nutrient-based soil, water, and sun.

Energy is the same. Energy needs to be filled with vitamins, minerals, and nutrients in order for it to make your body feel good. These healthy vitamins, minerals, and nutrients that fuel energy in a business are called mindfulness, compassion, forgiveness, creative expression, truth, integrity, and responsibility. High-character values are the nutrients that create the energy substance people need to feel good and live healthy. Without them, our bodies respond with physical pain, obesity, and a greater feeling of hunger. Rich, nutrient-based energy can only come from physically connecting with people who choose to live high-character values.

Technical Interference

We can't talk about human connection without addressing technology. We live in a world where information is instantaneous. Anytime we have a question, our first step is to "Google it." (I love how Google has figured out how to turn their business into a verb.) People use the Internet for everything, because everything is at our fingertips the minute we type a word. In fact, Google is so smart that you don't even have to finish the word and it already tells you what you're looking for. It's amazing. That being said, this wondrous world of instantaneous information has created an expectation of instantaneous response. We used to send an e-mail and expect a response back in 24 hours. Then we wanted it by the end of the day, and then within a few hours. If that's not good enough we send a text and expect an instantaneous response. We even get irritated if our text isn't acknowledged within the first five minutes after we hit send. Wow, are we even allowed to go to the bathroom anymore? Nope. Take your phone with you!

Let me be clear. I think instant information is wonderful, and I love how productive, efficient, and effective technology has allowed business to become. However, our society has become addicted to technology and being connected to instant information. I don't know about you, but I have literally turned the car around, driven 20 minutes out of my way, and missed a meeting, just because I forgot my phone at home. What's really funny is that I wasn't even expecting a call, a text, or an e-mail. I just felt naked without my phone. Yep, naked. And I was scared that I just *might* miss something if I didn't have my smartphone attached to my hip. I've done this more than once, even though I've had my laptop and tablet with me the whole time. Even with all the other supporting technology, I was still freaked out that I didn't have my trusty life companion right by my side. Interesting; I said *companion*. I believe that word is quite appropriate for the average person in today's world.

In today's society, technology has become our companion. We look for love online, entrench ourselves in social media, and text constantly. It's now okay to have meaningful conversations via text—those conversations are called *textersations*. The average business professional sends and receives a total of 115 e-mails per day—that's a lot of e-mail. People spend, on average, 30 percent of their workday just reading and responding to e-mail. Globally, people spend an average of 16 hours per month just surfing the web; in the United States alone, that average jumps to 32 hours per month. U.S. desktop users spend an average of 6 hours every month on Facebook; mobile users 11 hours. And if you're a gamer, you spend on average of 90 minutes per day online gaming. If you do the math, the average business professional spends up to 38 hours per week online—it's a full-time job. And that's just the average. If you're above average that number may be significantly higher. (The figures in this paragraph were taken from The Radicati Group, Inc., McKinsey Global Institute, Go-Gulf Web Agency, ComScore, and MyRealGames.com.)

The resounding conclusion is that most people's companion in life is their smart phone, laptop, or tablet. I'm not sure why everyone's online looking for love; their phone is right there! Who needs human interaction? You just need Google...until you find yourself exhausted, energy-depleted, and starving for human attention, for someone to actually talk to you, look at you, and be completely engaged in conversation *with* you, so you can feel their energy through their voice, their eyes, or their touch, and know that you're valued and accepted. That, my friend, is really what the Human

Energy Crisis feels like. Even though we're connected to everyone and everything, we're starved and alone, because in actuality we're connected to nothing human. People aren't stopping long enough to experience the one thing that is the source of healthy energy: true human connection.

Our addiction to technology and our inability to be present are major roadblocks to attaining healthy energy because people make technology and electronic connection a priority over human connection. The solution is not to do away with technological advances, instantaneous information, and paperless operations. In fact, all of those elements are highly beneficial, as long as they don't strip people and the business of healthy energy. If you want your business to thrive on healthy energy, and you want an energy ecosystem that ignites profitable action, you need to make building genuine relationships a priority over technology for everyone in the business. This means that, during meetings, people turn technology off and engage in conversation. Unless you're the one taking notes for everyone, close the laptop. This means that during one-on-one conversations, people aren't texting, checking e-mails, and answering phone calls that don't qualify as an absolute emergency. And if you're in the building when a meeting occurs, you show up and choose to be present, rather than pretending you're a telecommuter. If you want healthy energy and to feel good again, you need to put human connectivity over technology—period.

I've had a number of clients come to me throughout the years with concerns that a person on their team, their boss, or another colleague they work with just doesn't seem to listen. They're frustrated, because even though they've asked their colleagues repeatedly through e-mail, text, and voicemail to do certain things, or respond in certain ways, nothing happens. They feel disrespected, devalued, and unappreciated. The comment is often, "Am I the only one in this world who actually cares? Do they even know I exist?" I always ask the same question in response: "Have you talked to them? Have you had an actual conversation? You know, the kind where two people sit down, sometimes over coffee, and have a conversation?" Their response is usually the same: "No. I haven't tried that approach yet." So I tell them, "Actual conversations can be magic. Maybe you should try the conversation thing first, before you go too far off the deep end. If you look in their eyes, and take the time to talk with them, as though they are another human being, you may actually get the response you're looking for."

Relationships

The sacral chakra shares the need for trust with the heart chakra. Unless people feel trust in their sacral chakra, balancing the heart chakra will not generate action. Trust for the heart chakra of your business creates freedom that turns ideas and vision into reality, because it allows people to give and receive compassion, permission, and protection to show up authentically. Trust for the sacral chakra of your business creates freedom for each person individually to feel value and acceptance in this world. It's only when a business is able to balance its sacral chakra that it will experience optimal performance and engagement from everyone in the business—because it's within the sacral chakra that action, passion, will, perseverance, and the desire to succeed exist.

The sacral chakra of your business is the home of relationships—human connection. Its balance and health is directly influenced by how people in your business relate to one another, and the quality of the relationships people have with one another. It's the most sensitive of all the chakra systems in your business, because it's directly tied to the emotional connection among every person in your business. If you took a picture of the sacral chakra of your business, you would see a web of thin lines connecting each person to one another, and each line would be covered with the emotion that each personal connection represented. When healthy and balanced, the emotions covering the lines are of value, acceptance, and understanding. A healthy sacral chakra conveys the message that, "I am free to breathe." When unhealthy and toxic, the emotions are fear of abandonment, threat to social status and financial security, and self-protection covered in defensiveness. An unhealthy sacral chakra conveys the message that, "I need to protect myself so no one can take any part of me away. I must stand on guard, shielding any true emotion I have so it's not abused, taken advantage of, or used against me. If I show my true self, I'm not safe."

Here's the reality: If you have adults working in your business, there's a high likelihood that everyone in your business has an unbalanced sacral chakra, unless they're intentionally working on balancing their own energy system. Every one of us has had an experience that, at some point or another, created the fear of opening ourselves up to the world. If you want an energetically healthy business that fuels profitable action, you need to intentionally create opportunities for people to build trusting relationships that prove to everyone that their previous experiences with untrusting relationships don't apply in your business. Your business needs to prove to everyone that they are emotionally safe.

Similar to most people in your business, I learned the importance of the sacral chakra the hard way. I grew up in a home with divorced parents, with a mom who had to work three minimum-wage jobs to keep the house going. I was the poster child for Generation X. My sister, brother, and I were the latchkey kids who took care of ourselves—it was just life. And similar to so many people, I grew up incredibly self-sufficient and independent, but feeling completely abandoned. Even though both of my parents were in my life, because of certain life circumstances I felt like I had been dropped off on the corner to survive on my own. That was when I first started protecting myself from abandonment. The brick wall started going up, because I was scared that if I loved someone completely, opened myself up completely, that person would leave, and I would be left on the corner alone. So why do that? That feeling sucks. So I decided not to let anyone in; that way, I could never get hurt. Problem solved.

This solution worked wonders for my career. I just pretended that I was okay, and carried on by overcompensating with confidence and zest for life—confidence that landed me great opportunity for a short while. Inside, I really did have a zest for life, and joy still wanted to come out, but that zest and joy were overshadowed by my fear of abandonment and held captive by my choice to cover myself with toxic self-protection. This choice turned what was authentically inside of me into false acts of emotion.

Time went on, and I continued doing what most people do: I pretended I was great. On the outside, I was all smiles, laughter, confidence, and joy; on the inside, I felt alone and desperate for someone—anyone—to actually love me. So, unbeknownst to me, I gravitated toward anyone who made me feel loved. And I gave them what I call "false love" in return. False love occurs when it appears that you're giving yourself to someone, but you're actually protecting yourself and covering the fear you have of letting anyone see who and what you actually are inside—fearful that if they see who you really are they won't like you, or worse, they won't love you. So this false love thing worked for me, I thought. I then found myself in an emotionally and sexually abusive relationship that added to my fear of letting anyone in. So as a solution, I created a thicker brick wall of self-protection. This time I made sure the wall was filled with cement that was guaranteed to keep everyone out. And it worked, just like the false love thing. Or so I thought. I left the relationship, with my brick wall surrounding me, and not surprisingly I felt increasingly more alone. Even though the world thought I was great, and people were all around me, I was alone and starved for love.

Years passed, which included a failed marriage, career ups and downs, and lots of degrees and certifications to prove to the world that I was indeed valuable and worth loving. I thought that maybe if I looked successful on the outside, people would want to take the time to truly understand me. I spent years showing everyone how smart I was, using intelligence as a way to feel as though I was valued and accepted. In business, that worked wonders for a while. Then one day, shortly after I decided to finally jump off the corporate ship and start my own business, I was hit over the head. Not that this epiphany couldn't have happened while I was working in corporate, but for me this wakeup call had to happen after I jumped. I had jumped with confidence, never doubting that I would be extremely successful—because I was "really smart and had experience that people value."

You can imagine how surprised I was when the business didn't work. *What the hell? What am I doing wrong? I'm following the textbook, and this baby should be running smoothly.* Here's what I learned: My business wasn't working because I wasn't building relationships. In fact, I didn't even know how. That was the problem. Who wants to do business with someone with whom they don't have a trusting relationship? Nobody. It's the same thing when you're working in a business. Who wants to work with or for someone with whom they don't have a trusting relationship with? Nobody. Learning this relationship thing was the only way I was going to get my business off the ground.

Here's where it got scary: Through experience and a hell of lot of conversations, I realized that the only way I was going to be able to build an authentic relationship with anyone was if I had an authentic relationship with myself first. Yikes! I didn't even *like* myself, and I sure as hell didn't trust myself, because I blamed myself for every negative experience I had throughout life. So I had to learn to own only what was mine, forgive myself and everyone else, and let go. I had to learn how to see value in myself, accept myself, and understand myself before I could expect anyone in this world to see value in me, accept me, and understand me. And I knew that only then would I be able to build authentic relationships based on trust.

This is where my journey began. Again, it wasn't rosy. I had to purge my emotional baggage in a healthy, productive way, chip away at my brick wall of self-protection, and choose to see everyone as a human being who hurts, loves, laughs, and is trying to make it through this world just like me. I had to come to a place where *I actually wanted* to learn how to receive healthy energy and trust myself. That was the scariest part, because choosing healthy energy meant that I had to show people who I really was inside. You see, people don't connect to you because of intelligence and superficial acts of emotion. They connect to you because of your vulnerability and your authentic desire to connect with them. Healthy energy is exchanged when two people are willing to be vulnerable to each other.

I chose to no longer see myself as a victim who needed to be protected from abandonment and hurt. I realized that people who choose to abuse and live dysfunctional lives are people who are scared to death of being vulnerable and feeling powerless—and that's not mine to own. So I learned to create healthy boundaries and to see other people in this world as human beings who hurt, laugh, and love, and who are trying to make it through this world just like me. From there, the rest of the principles of this book started to fall into place. I became good at building authentic relationships, and my business started to thrive. You see, we are all born to connect. We walk through this life in synchrony with every other human being in this world. Energetically healthy relationships are how we live life to its fullest and enjoy each moment, but it's the healthy relationship we have with ourselves that are most important.

If you want an energetically healthy business that ignites profitable action, you need to fully understand and embrace the fact that every person in your business has his or her story. The story every person brings into the business impacts how they see themselves in the web of relationships that exist throughout your business. To build a healthy and successful energy ecosystem, you need to create intentional opportunities for people to see value in themselves and others, accept themselves and others, and understand themselves and others. That means people in your business have to have a healthy relationship with both themselves and everyone else in the business. You do this by implementing all the practices in this book, making frequent conversation a requirement, and creating opportunities to share stories and become vulnerable to one another. You see, when it comes to building relationships with yourself and others in the business, you have to build an operating system that honors the human element of your business. The human element of your business can only be honored if you're willing to listen to other people's stories and share your own.

Leadership Transparency

When it comes to Principle #7, leadership transparency is not about the general communication messages that are presented in your business; that element of business transparency was covered in Chapter 2. When it comes to human connectivity, leadership transparency is all about the one-on-one relationships you have with people in the business. Transparency is about showing up authentically to everyone, sharing your story respectfully, and allowing people to see you as a human being.

So often people make the comment that leaders don't appear human. The leaders who do appear human become liked by all and respected by all, and generate a following of people who want to work for them no matter what area of the business they're leading. People want to know their leaders are human. Remember the example of the neuralyzer in the Introduction? For many leaders, it's as though someone is standing at the doors of the business waiting to zap them with a neuralyzer when they walk through, saying, "You will not remember anything that makes sense for how to run a business in the current world." This example often applies when people take on leadership roles when they're not ready. It's amazing; you can take the smartest people in existence, put them in a leadership role when they're not ready, and—voilá—they forget how to be human. They know they're human, most of their peers know they're human, but the perception everywhere else in the business is that they are anything but human. The perception of leaders not being human is incredibly harmful to the business, because people only connect to other people who show their vulnerability and have a genuine desire to be in a relationship with other people. If you have leaders who don't even take the time to genuinely talk to people, they are choosing to fuel your business with toxic energy.

Transparency is about connecting with people and showing that you're a kind human being through your words and actions. No one will actually follow you if you don't show them that you're a human being who cares. If they do, it's out of fear, and they will leave your leadership as fast as possible and never look back. Being transparent means sharing your story and asking to hear other people's stories. Being transparent is about asking people genuine questions about them personally and inquiring about their opinion because you care. If you're thinking, *I don't care*, then you don't belong in a leadership role. If you don't care, you're not ready to be a leader.

Being transparent about who you are and showing that you're a human being who cares is the number-one priority for all leaders—period. It's the leaders who value, accept, and understand people of all diversities who successfully lead people forward. It's the people in leadership roles who don't care who are dumping unhealthy energetic toxicity into every corner of your business. If these toxic leaders choose to remain dysfunctional, and you choose to keep them in leadership roles, you are choosing to destroy your business, or, at the very least, to remain on a path of exhaustion, because the business will continue having an uphill battle to attain any type of performance metric.

Diversity

In Chapter 6, diversity was addressed within the personal power practice of *accepting nothing less than respect*. Discrimination is still everywhere in business, and until every human being in your business treats every other human being in your business with respect, toxic energetic cancer will continue to spread, harming everything in its way. Everyone needs to respect each other throughout the business because respect is the gateway to human connectivity.

Human connectivity is the source of energy. It's impossible to connect with another human being unless you are able to let go of the fear and restrictive thinking that creates unhealthy discriminatory boundaries. If you can't let go, then you are choosing to live with unhealthy energy that will continue to harm you. The solution? Everyone in the business needs to embrace diversity at all levels. Everyone needs to come to a place where they value, accept, and seek to understand one another regardless of differences. Instead of fearing one another, people need to support one another. Instead of making excuses that are intended to overshadow discrimination and judgment, people need to own their fears and restrictive thoughts, so they can overcome them and arrive at a place of mutual respect. People in your business need to know they can show up exactly as they are, beautiful in their own skin.

The Process: People First, Own Your Story, and Do No Evil

To have a successfully flowing energy ecosystem, the sacral chakra of your business needs to be balanced and circulating healthy energy. To do this, your business needs to make the human element of business a priority over technology and standard operating systems. I'm not in any way saying that technology and standard operating systems aren't important, but when it comes to creating energy that ignites action, people have to come first—period. Making the human element the priority means that building good relationships, developing leadership transparency, and respecting diversity become core drivers in your business. It's only then that true human connection is possible. The process for balancing the sacral chakra of your business includes incorporating three policies into daily operations:

1. **People First.**

2. **Own Your Story.**

3. **Do No Evil.**

Human connectivity is the source of energy. If you want a business that thrives on healthy energy, then you need to make sure that everyone in your business can connect to each other in healthy, meaningful ways—an intention that each policy makes crystal clear.

People First

The **People First** policy has three elements:

1. *Put away the technology, and don't use technology to intentionally avoid human contact.* Put away the laptop and be part of the meeting. Don't pretend you're a telecommuter when you're actually in the building. Unless it's an absolute emergency, don't check texts or e-mails or answer the phone while you're having a conversation with another person. All of these scenarios are rude, and become obstacles in building relationships and energetically connecting with other people.

2. *Have scheduled conversations frequently with all the people you work with, including one-on-one conversations with the business leader at least once a week.* Require people to have phone conversations, meet in person whenever possible, and get together as a team. This does not, in any way, imply that you remove your results-only work environment. This policy simply states that human contact needs to be made a priority for everyone when at all possible.

3. *Ask people questions, seek to understand their opinions, and physically show people that you care—this message is specifically for the leaders of the business.* The only way you will ever build a trusting relationship with your team is if you actually care about the people who are on your team. Caring

means that you ask them questions about them personally—not just about work-related topics. Get to know everyone personally. Be people's friend. Yes, you can be someone's friend and leader at the same time. Gone are the days when you had to separate yourself from everyone once you became a leader. In fact, if you separate yourself, you are fueling the business with negative energy, because healthy energy can only exist when healthy relationships exist.

Own Your Story

We all have a story, and everyone needs to be proud of their story and the lessons it has taught along the way—no matter what they are. Our story is who we are, and sharing our story with each other is how trusting relationships grow. Now let me be clear: When your business makes Own Your Story a policy, you will not have people rushing forward to share their story. That's fine, because that's not the point. The policy is Own Your Story, not Share Your Story. The policy makes the statement that everyone brings value to the business, and that their story is what makes them uniquely important. If people choose to share their story with other people, fantastic; if the policy simply reinforces the fact that they're valued and accepted, and that people want to understand them, that's great too. Either way, the Own Your Story policy starts to create opportunities for people to build relationships with themselves and others.

Just by making the statement, *Own Your Story*, and making it visible throughout the business, people will start thinking about their story, and thoughts that were hibernating will start to surface. Personal issues will come to the forefront, and the business will have created an opportunity for people to heal their emotional wounds. If this sounds scary, it's not. This will not impact the business negatively; in fact, it will have the opposite effect. It's guaranteed that people will start talking with each other, supporting each other, and becoming closer friends. Making an energy practitioner available to people onsite is a great way to support everyone on their journey.

Do No Evil

Google quickly became one of my favorite businesses when I found out about their "don't be evil" policy. Every business needs to incorporate this policy into everything it does—period. This policy is straightforward, and will no doubt fuel your business with healthy energy. Here it is: Do No Evil. That's it. Don't do anything evil, ever. This applies to anything a business does that impacts employees, consumers, the environment, and communities of any kind. Do No Evil. If the action is harmful in any way to anyone or anything, it's evil. Don't do it.

The Do No Evil policy applies across the business as a filter for any and all decisions, at any and all levels of the business. It's particularly important when it comes to diversity. If people in your business are treating other people poorly, and limiting others' opportunity because of their gender, sexual orientation, ethnicity, belief system, or any other individual right, that's Evil. I get that in today's world we have legal HR practices that try to limit discrimination in the workplace, but discrimination is still everywhere, and it needs to be stopped. The Do No Evil policy is a message to everyone in the business that treating people poorly and making judgments on other human beings because they don't fit into the box you've created for your own life is evil, wrong, and uncalled-for. And in a business that thrives on healthy energy, there is absolutely no room for evil behavior. That includes evil behavior from part-time Joe all the way up to the CEO.

Discrimination is a deep-rooted issue, and may require specialized training from a diversity expert. If this applies to your business, you need to hire outside support to help your business get to the root of your diversity issues, so you can start moving forward with building your healthy energy ecosystem. If you don't, circulating healthy energy is not possible, because discrimination and judgment will take down healthy energy like the plague.

Bottom line? Evil is not acceptable—ever—and if evil decisions are made, the consequence is easy: The person who made the decision, the people who agreed to the decision, and anyone who took part in putting the evil decision into action needs to experience severe consequence that should include termination from the business. Again, this goes far beyond the handbook policies, because the handbook is just a book of policies that usually no one reads. The Do No Evil policy needs to permeate the entire business so people see it, feel it, and live it. Thank you, Google, for paving the way, and proving that a billion-dollar business can still keep humanity at the core of its operation. Gone are the days that size can be used as a justifier for harmful business practices. Keep up the good work, my friends.

So here's the deal: If you want healthy energy to circulate through your business you need to make these three policies official. Put the policies in the handbook, on the intranet, on artwork throughout the business—put them everywhere. Again, these three policies need to be seen, felt, and lived by every person in your business.

Chapter Highlights

✳ **Human connectivity is the source of energy.**

✳ We are all one and interconnected through energy. We feel what's going on around us, and the result is either inspiration or depletion. Sitting at the sacral chakra of the business, the home of emotion and relationship, business transparency fuels this energy center.

✳ When the sacral chakra of your business is balanced, people feel valued, accept change easily, and are motivated to act in ways that drive profit.

✳ We are born to connect. Regardless of belief or spiritual understanding, one commonality exists among every human being on this planet: We are born to connect.

✳ Filling your business with energy frequencies created by high-character values is like filling your business with healthy electrolytes that give people an extra boost to their body.

✳ Addiction to technology and inability to be present are roadblocks to attaining healthy energy because people make technology and electronic connection a priority over human connection.

✳ It's only when a business is able to balance its sacral chakra that it will experience optimal performance and engagement from everyone in the business. This is because it's within the sacral chakra that action, passion, will, perseverance, and the desire to succeed exist.

✳ Transparency is about connecting with people and showing that you're a kind human being through your words and actions.

✳ The process for balancing the sacral chakra of your business includes incorporating three policies into daily operations: People First, Own Your Story, and Do No Evil.

Principle #8

Humanity Is the Future

Humanity sits within the root chakra of your business, where the basic human needs of people are met, and physical safety and financial security are provided. When the root chakra of your business is open and clear, people are financially secure, physically safe, stable, and present—not flaky, or as though they're floating through life. A strong root chakra in your business strengthens people's ability to carry on conversations with concentration "in the moment" and manage basic details of their physical existence such as completing daily tasks, keeping schedules straight, and showing up to

The root chakra of your business has a direct tie to the high-character value of responsibility. Responsibility is the value that's about inspiring and driving action by taking ownership for personal choices, admitting mistakes and failures, embracing the responsibility for serving others, and leaving the world a better place. When people live the high-character value of responsibility, deadlines are met, promises are kept, and the overall performance of the business improves.

The root chakra is the final component of your healthy energy ecosystem. This business chakra is the home of social responsibility and collective responsibility. It's here that your business takes care of the basic human needs of every person in your business and every community throughout the world. The mantra of the root chakra is **"We are all energetically connected, we are all one, and we all have a responsibility to take care of each other and the world in which we live."** People are fueled with healthy energy when they are given the opportunity to be part of something greater than themselves. Your business has a responsibility to provide that opportunity. If you want a business that energizes people, ignites action, and drives profit functionally, then you need to honor collective responsibility and collective strength, and build sustainable internal and external social responsibility programs that matter to everyone in the business and throughout the world.

Collective Responsibility

Energetically we are all connected, we are all one, and so we have a responsibility to each other. If you want healthy energy in your business, you can no longer live in the delusion that we are *not* all connected as one. Science has proven we are connected. Science has proven that energy exists inside, through, and all around us, connecting our thoughts, words, actions, and emotions. Collective responsibility means that we honor our connection with everyone in the business, we honor our responsibility to help each other, to support each other, and to move forward together, and we look at each other as human beings who hurt, love, and laugh just like us. Collective responsibility means we look at each other as people who are just trying to make it through this world by living the purpose they know to be their own truth. Our world can no longer live separately—that would destroy us. And in the short term, if your business does not live as a collective, you and everyone in your business will continue to suffer from the energy crisis, because human connectivity is the source of all energy.

Let me be clear: This does not mean people are not unique individuals, with unique stories, talents, and life aspirations. This also does not mean that people should be expected to become uniform and fit into a box where everyone looks, acts, and thinks the same. Collective responsibility is exactly the opposite: It means everyone in the business respects everyone for their individuality, and because of that respect, people are able to open themselves up fully to working, supporting, and living together as one. Collective responsibility means that you lift up people's individual strengths, and you see them as a significant value to the business regardless of their role. Collective responsibility means that everyone in the business matters, and everyone's opinions, comments, likes, dislikes, and stories are seen as success factors.

Years back, I had a mentor who shared with me one of the most valuable lessons in my career to date. She said to me, "If you always expect people to do well, if you always inherently believe people will do well, and if you tell people they will do well and that you believe in them, people will begin to believe in themselves, and they will inevitably do well." Collective responsibility is about believing everyone will always do well. It's about setting high expectations with the core understanding that everyone will actually meet them—an understanding that becomes truth, because, in a business that thrives on collective responsibility, people choose to come together, with all their individual strengths, to reach new worlds. In a business that has collective responsibility embedded in the essence of who and what it is, everyone will succeed because no one will let anyone fail—that is collective responsibility.

Here's a quote that brings collective responsibility and energy to life. The quote is from Barbara Brennan, a physicist who began teaching and working in the field of energy after she saw the healing power energy had on the human body. She said, "The whole universe appears as a dynamic web of inseparable energy patterns.... Thus we are not separated parts of a whole. We are a Whole."

Collective Strength

Collective strength is the energy generated from a business that has collective responsibility as a fundamental principle, and it's the power that specific energy has on the world. Remember the butterfly effect from the Introduction? Energetically, our individual thoughts, actions, and emotions have the power to cause a natural disaster on the other side of the world, or to create beautiful change that our world so desperately needs. The proof of collective strength showed up in my life when my ex-husband, one of my favorite people in this world, battled his cancer and won. Here's the story of how energy came into my life, and how I came to know the power of collective strength.

I woke up reluctantly at 7 a.m., having to go to a weekend class I had signed up for two months prior because I thought it would be fun. I was not feeling the fun when my alarm clock went off that morning. My mom came over to watch my daughter, and also to push me out of bed and convince me that I would be happy I spent an entire weekend at this "energy session" called Reiki. I was less than thrilled. Operating off of maybe three hours of sleep from taking care of my 9-month-old who still had not mastered the art of sleeping, working full-time running a new consulting business, finishing graduate school, and trying to manage a marriage that was less than smooth, I was exhausted.

It was that day, in the Reiki class, that I saw energy for the first time—and I *got* it. Let's be clear: I got it *not* because I was told about it, but because I experienced what it felt like for my body, mind, and soul to be infused with what I desperately needed in that moment: a jolt of juice. I physically felt the warmth and comfort of light in every part of my being, simply by having someone else place their hands on my body. My exhaustion dissipated, and it was replaced with a feeling of being alive—a feeling that had been absent from my life for quite some time.

In the years that followed, I practiced Reiki with friends and family, but never made energy work a primary focus of my life. I completed graduate school, got divorced, and started to embrace a new life. My work with corporate leaders continued to thrive; I was working with Fortune 500 clients, making great money, pulling myself out of extreme debt, buying a house in the ideal neighborhood, and making a life for myself and my daughter that most people would consider well-accomplished. With a life filled with activity and change, I kept energy work at arm's length.

Then I got a call when I was in Las Vegas, presenting at a convention. My ex-husband, James, had been diagnosed with cancer. It was enough to shake anyone's reality, and force you to question your existence. Our worlds changed instantly. Let me tell you, it doesn't matter how much baggage exists in a relationship, all hardships disappear in the moment you're faced with the potential of death. The baggage is replaced with love, compassion, forgiveness, and trust.

James had had a tumor the size of a melon, sandwiched between his ribs and the aortic valve of his heart, removed through chemotherapy treatments and surgery. Weeks later, James had the standard tests to make sure everything was okay, and the results showed the cancer was back. And this time, it was pissed off. James was then diagnosed with a rare form of testicular cancer that happened to be in his chest again. This rare form of cancer had a 20-percent survival rate—and that only with stem cell treatment, which only two places in the nation had the ability to administer. So James and his wife, Erin, another one of my favorite people in this world, packed their bags and moved into Manhattan's Hope Lodge. Together they were battling one of the ugliest wars of our time: cancer. Their only weapons were belief, hope, and incredible determination that they would win.

During his cancer treatment, many things became clear to me. The greatest clarity came with the understanding that I had no control—a concept that I believed to be foreign in my life. One day, feeling numb in the midst of change and spiritual questioning, I went for a walk. I was feeling a tug that there was something else I was called to do in this life, and I was absolutely frustrated and impatient because I couldn't figure it out. Many walks followed in the coming weeks, in which I felt my loss of control, asked my questions of existence, and a desperate sought for guidance. One of those walks put me on the journey that has brought me to all of you.

It was a cold, rainy day. I decided to brave the weather and take a walk to the lake. Up ahead I saw a bank of storm clouds covering the sky in the exact direction I was walking. The clouds turned me in the opposite direction, and I headed back up the neighborhood streets to a little shop that said CHAKRA CLEARING. Before I could think twice, I was on a table once again being introduced to this thing called energy. Remembering my experience five years prior, I was filled with the same warm comfort that re-energized my mind, body, and soul.

I left the shop that day, awake, present, thinking clearly, and more productive and motivated than I had felt in years. This experience took my current knowledge of energy work to a whole new level. I thought, *I feel amazing!* I kept going back to the shop, and the feeling kept getting stronger. Not only was I feeling better, but my creativity also started opening up in ways I couldn't explain. I had a sense of courage and strength brewing inside of me, motivating me to begin making life decisions that opened doors of opportunity.

Let's get something straight: My experience has created a strong personal belief in energy, but I am a woman who likes data and proof. And contrary to my larger-than-life personality, I think in term of process, systems, and strategy—a business mind through and through. I wanted to know how and why energy was having such a profound impact on my life, so I started to research energy work more deeply. From Einstein, Barbara Brannan, and Judith Orloff to Eastern practices that have impacted humanity for millennia, I immersed myself in the science and experience of energy.

My research led me to this final conclusion: Energy, as noted in the Introduction, is the vibrational frequency that everything made of matter puts *into* this world and *receives from* this world. Energy is like exhaust fumes or the steam off a freshly baked apple pie; you can't see the smell but it's everywhere, evoking emotions and actions of either disgust or delight. Just like a smell that fills a room, we all give off energy that creates emotions and actions that fills our reality.

Energy is inside us and all around us. Einstein said it best: "Everything is energy and that's all there is to it. Match the frequency of the reality you want and you cannot help but get that reality. It can be no other way. This is not philosophy. This is physics." You are energy, and your reality is the energy you're giving the world. Proof of energy, and the power it has to positively change our realities, is all around us. I witnessed this reality when James had thousands of people praying for his life, together amplifying their healing energy into the direction of one man—thousands of people coming together as a collective, creating a collective strength of healing energy. The energy didn't just stop with the prayers. I was in awe, seeing a man exhibit so much strength against all odds, knowing his only moments of comfort came while undergoing energy-work treatments—services hospitals are now providing to patients because Western medicine is finally beginning to understand that the Eastern healing modalities work.

Erin also saw the power of energy. One night when James was in incomprehensible pain, she remembered an energy healing technique one of the practitioners at the Hope Lodge had taught her, and decided to try it. She said, "It actually worked. It seemed like his pain was lessened, and for the first time that night, he appeared comfortable." After the battle of a lifetime, James is now part of the 20-percent club. I call that energy-based survival, and proof that the collective strength of energy has the power to save lives and change our world.

Energy is not just available to cancer patients or those experiencing significant challenges in their lives. It's available to everyone, at any time, anywhere. When it comes to energy, you're the one in control. In fact, your energy is the only thing in this world you can actually control—contrary to what you might think. Research continues to prove that practices dedicated to improving energy flow impacts the aging process, vitality, focus, well-being, and stress. Not surprising that my energy research led me right back to business.

Internal Social Responsibility

It's fascinating to me how often I receive the same response when I ask executives their definition of social responsibility. They say, "Social responsibility includes all of our efforts to take care of the world and our communities where we live and work." Great! I say, "Tell me more." They follow up with a beautiful list of all the ways the company is making or hopes to make an impact outside the four walls of the business. Again, great! "Your heart is in the right place," I say. "Tell me more." This is where I get the blank looks.

Do you know what's missing from businesses' usual definition of social responsibility? I have asked this question hundreds of times, and the same thing is always missing. Regardless of the size of the business, the amount of money available to social responsibility efforts, and how passionate executive teams are about social responsibility, the same thing is always missing. Have you figured it out? **"Our people"** is what's missing. Businesses get so wrapped up in taking care of everything outside their four walls that they often forget about their own people. They forget that the most important community to take care of is the community inside their four walls. You see, if businesses put the same care and intent toward their own people as they do in taking care of the rest of the world, then our communities, our businesses, and, yes, our world, would be stronger and healthier. If the people inside the business are taken care of, they'll have the strength, energy, and desire to take care of their communities when they leave at the end of the day.

Your business may provide benefits, and may even have a wellness program—those are all good, but they're only a start. If you want to fuel your business with healthy energy, you need to start taking care of people right down to their most basic needs. Taking care of people's basic human needs is how you balance the root chakra of your business. You need business systems that fairly and compassionately address the need for security of people's bodies, employment, resources, morality, families, health, and property. You see, these are the needs that are threatened in today's world, and are already missing from so many people's lives. This threat to basic human needs wreaks havoc on people's emotional system. These negative emotions are dumping toxic energy into your business, so your business, if it wants to circulate healthy energy, has a responsibility to help alleviate these threats for the greater good of your people.

Employment, Family, and Resources

Employment, family, and resources all go together in a package that requires one thing: money. We need money to exist in this world. The voice that communicates this basic need sounds like this: "I need to feel secure in knowing that I have the funds to provide food, shelter, and warmth for myself and my family." The world of business is full of mergers, acquisitions, and downsizing, and the basic need of employment is the most challenging for businesses to support. However, there are a couple of basic things over which every business has control: fair pay and responsible operations.

Fair pay means just that: You need to pay people fairly. If you have two different people in the same position, doing the same job, responsible for the same initiatives, pay them the same starting salary. If you have people being paid completely different salaries when they start, that's not fair pay; that's evil. It doesn't matter how well one person negotiated. If you pay people differently for the same exact role, it's evil, and as you know, your business needs to Do No Evil. You might be thinking, *Experience, education, and performance play a role when it comes to pay.* Yes, all of those factors should be considered when offering someone a position in the business. And yes, people should be also be rewarded for great performance. So here's the deal: Figure out all those initial factors, and then determine the salary at which *everyone* starts when they accept the role, and only hire people that fit those determining factors. Hiring exceptions can be made, but people still need to start at the same salary that everyone else received upon accepting that role.

I've worked with countless businesses that have multiple people doing the same exact job, yet making different salaries. In those instances some people are making thousands less than others, because the person making the hiring decision felt that one of them deserved a higher salary. In professional roles, I've seen salary variances upwards of $100,000—that doesn't even begin to address the realities at the executive level. I've seen businesses try to get away with "salary bands" that justify a $30,000 swing for the same job that required the same experience and education. This has even become a game—I've played it. Here's what you do. You accept a role and, while in the role, have a few conversations with friends to figure out the top salary for the position you hold. Then you perform really well for a while—let's say you do this high-performance thing for a year, sometimes less, then quit. A few months later, you say that you changed your mind, negotiate for the top salary, and voilá—you're now the top paid professional in that role. This happens everywhere, in every industry, and at every level.

Salary ranges create an emotion of resentment from those being paid less that festers like a bad disease, and negative energy continues to be dumped into your business. If you're not offering equal financial packages for everyone in the same role, you're discriminating. It doesn't matter what the "salary bands" say, or what industry standards indicate—they're wrong. Do No Evil. Don't discriminate. Honor fair pay by paying people who are in the same role the same salary. If you don't, you are choosing to pump negative energy throughout your entire business.

The second thing every business has control over is managing the internal operations responsibly. Yes, revenue and other top-line growth metrics are important, but how you manage the internal operations dictates how much money a business actually makes (profit). Energetically healthy businesses manage their internal operations responsibly. Leaders are generous yet fiscally responsible. Everyone in the business understands how their role genuinely impacts performance levels, and everyone takes responsibility for their performance. When challenges arise (because they always do), the business looks to the collective body to help come up with sustainable solutions, rather than relying on boardroom discussions with a select few leaders.

Morality

Again, this is where the Do No Evil policy comes into play. At the core of their being, people need to know that they're not being asked to do something that is morally and ethically wrong. This includes but is not limited to dumping chemicals into our oceans, waterways, and soil, discriminating against or putting judgment on other people, and lying about anything in order to cover someone else's ass.

Health and Body

Obesity, workplace stress, and chronic disease are literally killing people in today's world. Most people in this world are unable to afford health insurance, they don't have the funds to purchase athletic memberships, and they never had the opportunity to be educated on how alternative care can actually prevent disease and physical ailments. This also describes a great percentage of people who are employed by businesses.

A business that is fueled with healthy energy is a business that provides the basic health and wellness resources for everyone working in their business. In an energetically healthy business, executives and people working full time do not get greater benefits than part-time Joe. Everyone in the business receives equal health benefits, and the benefits are enough to make sure everyone's basic human need of health security is covered. Let me be clear. Everyone in this world has a responsibility to take care of his or her body—we only have one. I also want to be clear that I'm not telling business owners they have to take on all the responsibility of health insurance and wellness education themselves. However, I am saying that energetically healthy businesses proactively own the responsibility of figuring out how to provide everyone in the business with knowledge and resources that ensure every person in the business has a sense of security for their health. That means that small businesses that can't afford health insurance partner with nonprofit resources that can help provide health security to everyone in the business.

The second element of health security is alternative healthcare. Energy work is highly successful in mitigating so many current health challenges, and it costs significantly less than traditional healthcare. Eastern energy practices work, so make energy work available to all people in the business. There's a reason why Barbara Brennan, a physicist, began her work in the field of human energy. She understands energy, and she understands that energy is the missing component to health and wellness everyone is looking for. It's right in front of you. Make it available to everyone.

There are millions of health and wellness programs available to businesses, but people's bodies, at the core of our existence, are only asking for three things:

1. Food that's not filled with chemicals and is good for the body.

2. Time throughout the day, week, month, and year when people feel they can rest without suffering repercussions.

3. Opportunity for everyone to get up and walk.

If your business wants healthy energy, if you want an ecosystem that energizes people and ignites profitable action, then the business has to provide these three things. You always see people shoving unhealthy food down their throats, eating while working at their desk, working triple-time during the week, and gaining weight because they don't feel the business has given them the freedom to operate any other way. If this isn't clear, and you don't completely understand the essence of giving freedom, re-read Chapter 5; balancing the root chakra of your business depends on it.

External Social Responsibility

Humanity is our future—we, human beings, are the future of this world. If we want a future, if we want future generations to have a future, we have to get serious about taking care of humanity. Everyone talks about world peace, attaining a sense of wellbeing, and improving the environment—everyone talks about it because we are all in a desperate need of healing. Our world has to change if we want a healthy future, and change will not happen until we get to the core of why hurt exists, and why humanity and our world are both suffering. People are broken, and until we mend the wounds, people will continue to take out their pain on the earth and on each other. Dysfunctional business practices are the cause of the hurt, and functional business practices are the solution.

Across the world, businesses have the collective power to change our existence for the better. Collectively (and some individually), businesses have enough money and talented people to overcome the massive hurt we've caused both the human race and the Earth. From taking care of individual people, to passing healthy global legislation and cleaning the waterways of our world, it's business that has the ability to make the change we so desperately need to make.

People have tumors throughout their bodies because of chemicals in our food. We can't swim safely in fresh water lakes because our water is, or is becoming, toxic. Our oceans are filled with garbage, and people all over the world can't get their food supply out of the oceans because fish are filled with toxicity. Global warming is real, and our Earth is experiencing extreme weather because she's in pain. We choose to put carbon into the atmosphere because oil makes money—even though we already have the technology to eliminate the need for harmful fuels.

Humanity is our future. If we are to create an Earth where peace exists, where people can actually drink water and eat food safely, where oceans aren't filled with chemicals, and where people can feel good again, then improving the health and well-being of humanity needs to be the core purpose of every business in existence. If it's not, dysfunctional people will continue to covet money as their harmful addiction, and they'll continue to make poor business choices based on that harmful addiction. The result of those dysfunctional decisions will be a world that no longer has a need for money—because humanity will no longer exist. We can have all the health and wellness programs we want, but until every business chooses to operate by the policy of Do No Evil, our world and all of humanity will continue to suffer.

You might be thinking, *You can't just blame business.* Yes, I can. Dysfunctional business *is* to blame. The whole world can blame dysfunctional business for the harmful state we're in, because it's truth. You see, it's pure economics: Business, government, and consumers together are driving dysfunctional business decisions. At face value, these three components of economics appear separate. In fact, you may say, "Consumer demand is what drives the goods and services businesses choose to produce. Consumers can just stop purchasing. Government is there to help balance and protect consumers from poor business practices, and to ensure the wellbeing of the people who live within its jurisdiction. Government can just shut business down." Sounds good on paper, but here's the reality: It makes no difference what side of economics you're on—business, government, or consumer—everyone's in bed with each other.

You see, dysfunctional businesses give dysfunctional government money as a form of persuasion. Government officials have stock in the businesses that make them money. This happens under the table and on top of the table all the time. Businesses have become master psychologists, and have figured out how to manipulate marketing efforts to increase consumer purchasing power for the benefit of selling their specific goods and services. Consumers have stock all over the place, and even though most people individually care about the world and they want to do good for humanity, there are many dysfunctional consumers who choose to invest their money in businesses that give them the greatest return on investment regardless of their evil business practices. Furthermore, consumers are choosing to give away their power and political rights because they're not choosing to educate themselves and actually use the rights and power they have. The metric of societal dysfunction is the GDP. There's a reason I took the time in the Introduction to define the word *business* as it pertains to this book. Here it is again: *Business* is a word that is applied to politics, religion, and private or public commerce. I use the word *business* to describe any entity trying to drive profits into the organization.

Here's the deal: It's not money that's evil. What's evil is the act of coveting money for power. Millions of people in this world are functional, energetically healthy, and have the power to change the existence of humanity and our Earth for the better. Amazing businesses throughout the world are making a positive difference every day—for-profit or not-for-profit, it doesn't matter. You see, money itself is beautiful, and we're going to need a whole hell of a lot of it to make this world healthy again. And our world and all of humanity *will* become healthy again. This is inevitable, because too many of us who are energetically healthy and powerful human beings are coming together with collective strength to change this world. Together, as a collective, we're entering this battle with passion and perseverance, and our only weapons are belief, hope, and determination that we will win.

If you haven't already, open your eyes, look around, get out of your microcosmic existence, and physically look at the pain that poor business decisions have caused our world. Then choose to change. Choose to become functional. Choose to put healthy energy back into this world. If you're someone whose eyes are already wide-open, thank you—and please continue to do everything you can inside your business to change this world in order to help humanity and our Earth feel good again.

The Process: Planting the Root Chakra

Following are the programs and policies that create a foundation for your energy ecosystem. The root chakra is just that: a root that needs to be firmly, securely planted in the ground, where it can provide life-giving energy to the business. People are the source of that life-giving energy, and the people in your business need to be taken care of.

An Internal Social Responsibility Plan

The mantra of the root chakra is "We are all energetically connected, we are all one, and we all have a responsibility to take care of each other and the world in which we live." People are fueled with healthy energy when they are given the opportunity to be part of something greater than themselves, and feel free to perform when they have confidence that their basic human needs are secure and provided for. The following policies and processes are designed to support the root chakra by creating an internal social responsibility program that fuels healthy energy throughout the business from the inside, and an external social responsibility program that allows the healthy energy of the business to flow throughout the rest of the world.

Internal Humanity Budgets

Internal humanity budgets are funds that provide leaders with the ability to take care of the people on their team during times of need. These are funds that someone in need can receive similar to the way a grant works: no strings attached. Example scenarios include someone finding out he is losing his house due to circumstances out of his control. Another example might be someone needing to put food on the table after finding out her child has terminal cancer. A humanity budget is designed to take care of the basic human needs of the people inside the business.

It's important not to make this complicated. The minute red tape gets involved, humanity budgets will become tainted with bad energy and complicated to disperse. The perceived hassle will automatically give leaders amnesia—they won't remember the budgets exist at all. So make it simple. Make it one lump sum per leader. Make the budgets known to everyone in the business. Don't micromanage it, and step away from the red tape. This is an exercise of trust, compassion, and freedom.

Community Barter Sites

A community barter site is an online program that allows people to confidentially request help in times of need, for themselves or for other people inside the business. The site is barter only, and allows everyone in the business to confidentially respond to the needs of others. Again, no strings attached. Barter items may include groceries, clothing, and school supplies. The intent of the initiative is to give people in the business a vehicle by which to help take care of one another when people need help the most. The confidentiality of the program makes it safe for people to participate without shame or guilt.

Fair Pay Policy

Fair pay means just that: pay people fairly. Different people in the same position, doing the same job, responsible for the same initiatives, need to be paid the same starting salary. If you have people being paid completely different salaries when they start, that's not fair pay. Yes, education and experience play a role in salary, so figure out all those initial factors, and then determine the salary *everyone* starts at when they accept the role, and only hire people that fit your determining factors. If hiring exceptions are made, that's great, but people still need to start at the same salary everyone else received upon accepting that role. Additionally, performance increases need to be results-based and determined by a formula that is fair and equal across the board.

Do No Evil Policy

I'm repeating this from Chapter 7 because it's so crucial: Do No Evil. That's it. Don't do anything evil, ever. This applies to anything a business does that impacts people working inside the business, consumers, the environment, and communities of any kind. Do No Evil. If the action is harmful in any way to anyone or anything, it's evil. Don't do it. The Do No Evil policy applies across the business as a filter for any and all decisions, at any and all levels of the business. And it's particularly important when it comes to diversity. If people in your business are treating other people poorly, and limiting people's opportunity because of their gender, sexual orientation, ethnicity, belief system, or any other individual right—that's *evil*. The Do No Evil policy is a message to everyone in the business that treating people poorly and making judgments on other human beings because they don't fit into the box you've created for your own life is evil, wrong, and uncalled-for. And in a business that thrives on healthy energy there is absolutely no room for evil behavior. That includes evil behavior from part-time Joe all the way up to the CEO.

Health Insurance and Alternative Care

In an energetically healthy business, executives and people working full time do not get greater benefits than part-time Joe. Everyone in the business receives equal health benefits, and the benefits are enough to make sure everyone's basic human need of health security is covered.

Secondly, energy work should be available to all people in the business. Energy is the missing component to health and wellness that everyone is looking for, and it's right in front of you. Make it available to everyone.

Organic Food, Fresh Water, and a Daily Walk

I was in an energy workshop one evening when I shared with the facilitator that I was doing everything that I needed to do energetically, but I was still so damn tired. Falling-asleep-in-the-middle-of-the-workshop kind of tired that night. She said to me, "Did you give yourself fresh food and water today? Did you take yourself out for a walk?" I just looked at her and said, "I'm not a pet. I'm a person." We both started laughing, and she said, "I'm serious. What would happen if you just left your pet cooped up without any fresh food or water, and then you decided that you didn't want to take it for a walk." I just looked at her again and said, "Oh my God, you're right. That would be horrible. And no, I haven't done any of those things." Then I started laughing again, and said, "Oh my God, I'm my own pet. I have to give myself fresh food and water, and take myself out for walks. That's the problem, I'm doing none of that." She was a genius. So I started treating myself like my own pet, and it worked. Amazing. Organic food, fresh water, and daily walks are magic.

Again, it's not rock science, but we have made health and wellness so complicated that most of the time we forget that to stay healthy and awake all we need is fresh food, water, and a walk. To circulate healthy energy in your business you need to make sure that organic food and fresh water are available to everyone, and that everyone finds time to take a walk. Make it fun, and start asking people if they've taken their number-one pet out for a walk that day. I guarantee they'll laugh, and laughter in and of itself fuels businesses with healthy energy. That brings us to the final internal social responsibility initiative: fun.

Just Have Fun

Okay, for all you business leaders out there who decided to take the word *fun* out of the business vocabulary, put it back in. No, seriously, don't be a joykill. Science has proven that laughter generates good energy. People become energized, full of life, and actually perform at higher levels when they're having fun and laughing. Fun is not the antithesis of professional—you can have both at the same time. If you deprive yourself and the business of fun, play, and laughter, you are depriving yourself and everyone in the business of the same healthy energy that drives profits.

Be careful, this is not the "fun committee"; don't turn fun into red tape. You can't force people to have fun. Don't try to create a process for fun and laughter—it doesn't work. Notice that I didn't put the words *policy*, *committee*, or *procedure* after the title, *Just Have Fun*. Here's how you have fun in the business: You just let it happen.

Don't get angry with people when they're laughing in the hallways, joking around in their office, or pulling a safe, harmless practical joke. Remember, there's a Do No Evil policy—their jokes won't do evil. Lighten up. People work incredibly hard, so let them have some fun.

✳✳✳

The list of internal social responsibility efforts can go on and on; feel free to add additional initiatives that meet the needs of the people in your business. If you have unique situations that require unique initiatives, go for it. Here's my only challenge to you: As you think about your internal social responsibility initiatives make sure you're thinking about how the business can respond to the basic human needs of everyone in the business—including the basic human need to laugh.

An External Social Responsibility Plan

Social responsibility is usually a significant topic in large businesses and less so in small business. That being said, external social responsibility needs to be a significant topic for *all* businesses regardless of size. From a one-person shop to a billion-dollar enterprise, every business needs to be focused on social responsibility. The following is an external social responsibility plan that a business of any size can leverage. The plan is guaranteed to fuel your business with healthy energy, and it's guaranteed to start improving the health and well-being of humanity and our world.

There are four critical success factors for your social responsibility program:

1. A dedicated committee.

2. A key sponsor with immediate decision-making authority.

3. Visible priority within the business.

4. No red tape.

A Dedicated Committee

Your business needs a dedicated committee that includes people from various levels and roles throughout the business. The committee needs to meet frequently, have a consistent agenda, champions for each element, and dedicated support for those champions. Committees can range from six to 12 people. Here is the key success factor for the committee: They must have the trust and freedom to run the program, and not have to jump through a hundred process and approval channels in order to move something forward. The committee needs the freedom to make immediate decisions in direct partnership with the sponsor.

A Key Sponsor With Immediate Decision-Making Authority

The program needs one key sponsor who has the ultimate authority in the business to make decisions without holding up any of the initiatives. If the sponsor is someone who has to go back to someone else to get approval for anything related to the program, the program won't work, because you've now created red tape. The sponsor may be an owner, a C-suite executive, a significant mid-level leader, or someone who has been given decision-making authority when it comes to managing the social responsibility P&L. One additional note on sponsors: whomever it is, he or she needs to be functional, present, and engaged in the program, and must have a passion for leading social responsibility initiatives. If all of those characteristics are not within a sponsor, the program won't work, and you'll end up with a ton of frustrated people and bad energy.

Visible Priority Within the Business

To be a *visible* priority, the social responsibility program must be one of the top three core initiatives of the business. You see, social responsibility programs, when done right, drive profits.

They drive profits because when people contribute to something greater than themselves, and they know they're making a difference in the world, their performance level increases, they become more engaged, and they want to maintain their loyalty to the business. Additionally, consumers want to purchase from businesses that are putting healthy energy into authentically helping the world, rather than unhealthy energy into marketing manipulation. That brings us to another critical success factor: *The social responsibility program cannot be intended as a marketing ploy.* The intention must be pure; if it's not it won't be sustainable because people, inside and outside the business, will figure it out and see the business as manipulative and deceitful.

No Red Tape

I love when I say, "No red tape," and business leaders respond with, "We need to have a process and a system to make sure people run the program appropriately. They're giving money; we don't give that authority to just anyone. We need an approval process, a funding process, a committee process, and a subcommittee process. If this is a top priority, we can't just have *anyone* on the committee, and we need layers of process." My response is, "No red tape. Trust your people, give them freedom, and let go. The program won't work with red tape, because it'll get bogged down with bureaucratic policy and decision-making processes, and nothing will move forward. You see, our world needs to change, and humanity doesn't have time for you to figure out how to get 50 signatures in order to process one decision that could have taken two minutes. Trust, give freedom, and let go." Giving trust and freedom to the committee is key, and if you're still uncertain about the concept of trust and freedom, re-read Chapter 5.

Within the energy ecosystem, your business needs to have a social responsibility program with one sole purpose: to improve the health and wellbeing of humanity. Within the program there are three elements:

1. Funding.

2. A partner SR business.

3. Mission trips.

The effort within each of these elements may vary depending on the size of the business, but the three elements always remain the same. As with creating a Destination Map for your business, having more than three initiatives causes a feeling of being overwhelmed, and efforts aren't sustained. These are the elements that will create a successful, sustainable social responsibility platform for your business.

Funding

The social responsibility program must be given a dedicated budget, and the committee, together with the sponsor, must be given the trust and freedom to immediately approve funding decisions. Funding decisions include:

1. Giving to a charitable business that falls within the scope of the program.

2. The cost of program mission trips.

Don't make this complicated. Those truly are the only two funding categories. The program is intended to partner your business with an organization dedicated to the specific program scope you chose—your Partner SR Business—so you don't have to worry about all the granular expenditures that go along with managing large social responsibility programs.

A Partner SR Business

Your first step is choosing a partner SR business. The beauty of this social responsibility program design is that your business is responsible for funding and hands-on support only. Your partner SR business is the expert administrator for all the details that go into making social responsibility programs happen. The role of your business is to financially support your partner SR business, get involved with hands-on volunteer opportunities, and, to quote Gandhi, "Be the change you want to see in the world."

The aim of the social responsibility program you and your partner SR business choose needs to fall within one of four key categories that address the root cause of the hurt both humanity and the Earth are experiencing. The categories are:

1. Clean water.

2. Clean land.

3. Alternative energy (not human energy).

4. Earth-friendly products and services.

You'll notice there is nothing about health, wellness, food, or even children. This is intentional because when we address health, wellness, and food as categories we're not addressing the *root* of the problem; we're only addressing the problem. Until we address the root of the problem, all other efforts become a Band-Aid, a defense mechanism, and a short-term fix. For example, yes, we want everyone to eat organic food, but if we keep dumping chemicals into our water, spraying and filling our land with toxins, and putting carbon into the air, in years to come organic food won't exist. This applies to medical advancements, pharmaceuticals, wellness efforts, obesity issues, and more. Let me be clear: I think all of those are worthwhile efforts, and I commend the businesses that are out there focusing on those categories, but those categories will not get to the root of the problem. When it comes to children, remember that this entire social responsibility plan is *for* children, because without this plan our children won't have an Earth to live on and their life expectancy will continue to decrease.

* ***Clean water:*** This category involves eliminating and preventing chemicals, garbage, and anything that is toxic in any way from being dumped into our oceans, lakes, and rivers. The category also involves cleaning our waterways and making sure humanity around the world has clean water to drink. Water is the life source for all of humanity. Next to energy, water is the greatest resource of our world.

* ***Clean land:*** This category involves eliminating and preventing chemicals, garbage, and anything that is toxic in any way from being sprayed or dumped into our soil, crops, and forests. This includes everything from toxic fertilizer to toxic landfills.

* ***Alternative energy:*** This category involves advocating for and influencing legislation, funding, and sourcing of alternative energy. We already have the technology needed to bring alternative energy to the market; now we need people to make alternative energy a non-negotiable for everyone in the world.

* ***Earth-friendly products and services:*** This category involves funding efforts and being part of innovation solutions for the development and distribution of products and services that are not harmful to the Earth. Consumers desperately need more Earth-friendly alternatives if we're going to improve the health and well-being of this world at the pace at which it needs to improve.

*

Mission Trips

A significant part of the social responsibility plan involves mission trips. The purpose is clear: to improve the health and well-being of humanity. The mission is chosen by the business in collaboration with the partner SR business, and will also be based on the program category (clean water, clean land, alternative energy, or Earth-friendly products and services) the business has chosen to support. The reason why mission trips are so incredibly important is that change—in people, communities, and the world—occurs through experience. Mission trips are about going out into the world to literally *be* the change.

One of the greatest life-changing experiences I've had to date was when I went on a two-week mission trip to Argentina, from Buenos Aires to Patagonia to Iguazu Falls. Argentina is not a wealthy country. It was at one time, but the country has suffered great economic hardship, and many people are still living in poverty. And yet, as a visitor, you would never know that was the case. Every person with whom I came in contact had a sense of life inside him or her that I had never seen before. I could look into people's eyes and instantly see and feel how much gratitude, appreciation, and love they had inside them. The people I talked with listened, asked questions, and cared enough to keep the conversation going, even though we didn't even understand the words that were coming out of our mouths. In fact, many conversations ended up with both of us just laughing, because we had no clue what was going on.

When the trip ended, we cried. In two weeks, amazing friendships had formed and no one wanted to leave each other. But we said our goodbyes, and in that moment I realized I was actually saying goodbye to who I was and hello to someone new. This was one of the experiences that ignited my acceptance of myself (the story I shared about my own life journey in Chapter 7). You see, here's what happened on that trip: When I looked into the eyes of these people who had nothing, I saw people who had everything. I saw life. And I realized that they were no different from anyone else I knew; *I* was the person who was different. For two weeks, I was immersed in a life without materialistic items, status, or money—those distractions were gone. I lived simply, because I didn't have a choice to live otherwise. And with everything stripped away I actually noticed life, and I noticed it inside another human being. I stopped long enough to see, feel, and experience what it meant to actually connect with another human being—and change happened.

I came back to the States a different person—a better person. I started to look at life differently. The experience was an igniter, and it put me on a path where I started to align my life with my values and my purpose, and it helped me begin to understand what it meant when someone said "authentic relationship." And I realized, once I was home, that if I stop long enough to look into someone's eyes, life always looks back into mine.

Mission trips are important, but not for the reason everyone thinks they're important. Sure, you physically help other people who need your help, and you have a significant impact on the world in amazing, tangible ways, but the real point of a mission trip, and the real change, is that you come back a different person—a person who begins to understand life. It's that understanding that has the power to open eyes, and it's that understanding that has the power to improve the health and well-being of humanity and change our world.

Chapter Highlights

* **Humanity is the future.**

* Improving the health and well-being of humanity is the only answer to preserving a world that will continue to fuel business.

* The root chakra of your business is where people's basic human needs are met, and physical safety and financial security are provided.

* The root chakra of your business has a direct tie to the high-character value of responsibility.

* Collective responsibility means that we honor our connection with everyone in the business, that we honor our

responsibility to help each other, to support each other, and to move forward together, and that we look at each other as human beings who hurt, love, and laugh just like us.

✳ Collective strength is the energy generated from a business that has collective responsibility as a fundamental principle.

✳ The mantra of the root chakra is, "We are all energetically connected, we are all one, and we all have a responsibility to take care of each other and the world in which we live."

✳ Internal responsibility is about taking care of people's basic human needs inside the business. You need business systems that fairly and compassionately address the need for security of people's bodies, employment, resources, morality, families, health, and property.

✳ Humanity is our future. If we are to create an Earth where peace exists, where people can actually drink water and eat food safely, where oceans aren't filled with chemicals, and where people can feel good again, then improving the health and well-being of humanity needs to be the core purpose of every business in existence.

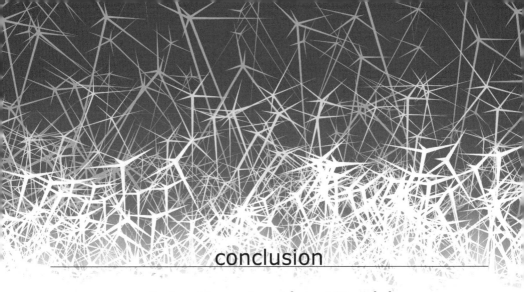

conclusion

A Letter to the World

Energy is all around us, and inside us. It moves through us, and is the one thing in this world that connects us with authenticity. Have you ever looked into someone's eyes and just known that you were accepted, loved, and respected? Have you ever stood in front of someone, and without any words at all, felt unbelievably connected. Even when you left the presence of that person, you could still feel him or her around you, as though you were one? Have you ever been around someone and had that feeling that words couldn't explain, but you knew it was right and good? These are the moments when you know that someone sees every part of you, and he or she loves and respects every part of you. This is the feeling of absolute trust that allows you to move forward, with an absolute knowledge that you are safe to finally be free. That's the power our energy has on the people standing in front of us, and that's the power our energy has on the world.

You see, energy has no judgment; it never discriminates, and it's available to everyone. Energy is how our thoughts and emotions travel through this world. It will never hide from anything, will never hide anything from you, and will always deliver the precise message the person in front of you is sending—even if that person is trying to hide it. To understand energy is to understand that everything in this world is transparent, and vulnerability is simply a personal statement to yourself saying that you actually want to see people for who they are, and you want to see the world for what it is: beautiful.

Businesses need to change. People are tired. Our Earth is hurting. We have everything in front of us right now to be the change we want to see in this world: money, technology, intelligence, and now understanding of the significant impact our energy has on the rest of the world; it's all in front of us, and we can no longer hide from the reality that we need to make this a better world. A world where everyone is accepted and respected, a world where water is clean, the soil can grow nutrient-rich food that's safe to eat, and people can buy things, travel, and take care of their families, while knowing they're not harming themselves or the Earth. People deserve to live a healthy life. You deserve to live a healthy life. This change needs to start within the very core of the problem, and it needs to start in the exact place the harmful dysfunction started: business.

So make it happen. Right now, make it happen, so you and the rest of the world can start waking up each morning being able to say, "It's a beautiful day."

appendix

The Energy Assessment

The energy assessment is designed to help your business identify where you have unhealthy energy, and what areas of the business need the greatest amount of attention and effort. The assessment is a great tool that can help you and your business determine how to prioritize initiatives as they relate to building your energy ecosystem. I encourage you to have everyone in the business take the assessment in order to get a valid gauge of your business's current energy level. A collective result is the only way you can get a true measurement of where the business is on the spectrum of healthy energy.

The intent of this book has been to help you build a functional energy ecosystem that fuels your business by energizing people, igniting action, and driving sustainable profits. To accomplish this, your business needs to operate by the Eight Principles of Business, which are directly aligned with your business chakra system. Each chapter has contained a process for attaining maximum healthy energy levels for your business, which I encourage you to re-read after you take the assessment, and begin implementing the process for areas where the assessment showed a deficiency. The assessment gives you a snapshot of the current state of your business, and the chapters give you a step-by-step roadmap for building your ecosystem. Trust the process, and know that building an energy ecosystem takes time, but the results are forever healthy.

Instructions

The assessment is broken into eight sections, with each section representing one of the Eight Principles of Business. There are 10 statements under each of the principles. Read each statement carefully and answer True or False for each of the statements. Make sure that when you're thinking about your response, you're thinking about the business as a whole, not just your specific experience. Additionally, choose the answer that most closely describes your business as it is now, not the way you or others wish it to be in the future.

Principle #1: Functional leaders drive profits.

Leader functionality is the key to unleashing human energy and driving profits. Sitting at the crown chakra of your business, leadership energy spills over into all aspects of the business, creating an environment that either fuels productive energy or breeds exhaustion.

_____ Leaders are more focused on C-suite, divisional, or owner direction than people.

_____ Leaders are showing their "worst" frequently or more than usual.

_____ Leaders have become frozen by politics, and/or are allowing politics to drive decisions even when better options exist.

_____ People are leaving the business or thinking about it.

_____ Engagement and retention levels in the business have declined or stayed mediocre.

_____ People have a tendency to blame others and make excuses for their mistakes rather than accepting ownership and taking responsibility.

_____ People feel that they can't make any decisions without receiving specific approval from management prior to doing simple tasks or taking care of customers.

_____ Gossip, behind-the-back conversations, complaining, and "don't repeat this" conversations are common in all levels of the business.

_____ Lunch is a rare privilege—unless being done while working.

_____ Twelve- to 14-hour days are not uncommon.

Total # of _T_s: _____

Principle #2: Vision and purpose ignite forward momentum.

Vision and purpose give people inside your business the guidance and wisdom to move forward. As the third eye chakra of your business, vision and purpose create clear thinking and the focus necessary to attain goals and aspirations.

_____ Everyone in the business clearly understands what the business wants to achieve in five years.

_____ The vision and purpose of the business is about more than money.

_____ The goals of the business are sustainable, and make sense in relation to the vision and purpose of the business.

_____ Everyone in the businesses feels valued because the vision and purpose of the business conveys the importance of each person in the business.

_____ The goals of the business are clear and attainable.

_____ The vision and purpose of the business makes people feel as though they are contributing to something greater than themselves because of working for the business.

_____ Everyone understands how the business is going to attain its vision.

_____ Everyone in the business can describe what the business will look like and feel like in five years.

_____ Everyone in the business clearly understand their role, because everyone was part of defining their role.

_____ Leaders share goals, and bring everyone in the business along on the journey.

Total # of *Ts*: _____

Principle #3: Truth and clarity motivate action.

Internal communication is the delicate balance of silence and words for the benefit of motivation. Internal communication lives within the throat chakra of your business, and it's within this energy center that the business needs to convey responsibility and decisions with clarity and truth.

_____ Every leader in the business shows up with positive intent.

_____ Everyone in the business understands how to manage their anger, and they are understanding of others' points of view.

_____ Communication throughout the business appears truthful and transparent.

_____ Vocal and written communication throughout the business appears straightforward and devoid of hidden agendas or implications.

_____ Leaders always stand up for what is right even in those moments when what is right isn't seen as favorable among executives and peers.

_____ Leaders always state their true intent and never appear manipulative or deceitful.

_____ Everyone in the business is asked for his or her input.

_____ The input that leaders ask for is always used to help better the business.

_____ Leaders follow up, do what they say they will do, and follow through on commitments.

_____ Everyone in the business is able to remain objective, name their emotions, respectfully state their needs, and make professional requests when needed.

Total # of *T*s: _____

Principle #4: People are driven to live out a purpose.

"I want to spread my wings and fly, be part of something greater than myself, and feel like I'm living my purpose." This is the voice of Principle #4. Sitting within the thymus chakra of your business, creating opportunity for people to become engaged in the business, on their terms, drives this energy center.

_____ Every person in the business can clearly communicate their personal values and life purpose.

_____ The business supports personal changes in roles and responsibilities in order for people to align with their personal values.

_____ The business encourages everyone in the business to share their values and life purpose with each other.

_____ Everyone in the business is actively supported in figuring out their values.

_____ Everyone in the business is asked to develop an action plan that is intended to align their business roles and responsibilities with who they are as individuals.

_____ The passions and strengths of everyone in the business are both respected and leveraged.

_____ It's clear throughout the business that the business respects the values of the people who work for the business.

_____ People's differences and strengths are celebrated in the business.

_____ Leaders ask questions and show interest in people's unique characteristics, and it shows.

_____ The business doesn't expect people to conform, and respects individuality.

Total # of *T*s: _____

Principle #5: Freedom turns ideas and vision into reality.

Ideas and vision are attained through attitude—also called an internal brand. Sitting at the heart energy center, the right business attitude is fueled by compassion, trust, and freedom. When a business has a healthy attitude, there's nothing it can't accomplish.

_____ My leader's behaviors help me feel as though I can express my ideas freely, openly, and without hesitation.

_____ The business's processes and systems help me to feel as though I can express my ideas freely, openly, and without hesitation.

_____ What my leader tells me is always true.

_____ The information the business communicates is always true.

_____ My leader and the business have my best interests in mind anytime decisions are made.

_____ My leader listens to me, and I know my leader hears what I say because he or she responds with genuine questions, comments, or beneficial concerns.

_____ My leader and the business always make me feel supported, and help me to know that I add value. I know this to be true because following up with commitments made is a priority that is always attained.

_____ The business environment allows me to freely make decisions, take care of clients, and implement new ideas in my own unique way.

_____ Every leader in the business shows compassion. The business leaders genuinely empathize with others, and show sympathy with authenticity.

_____ The business environment makes me feel safe and protected emotionally; I completely trust that my leader's response to my ideas will not cause me to feel shame, hurt, or guilt.

Total # of *Ts*: _____

Principle #6: Creative expression fuels change and growth.

Change and growth are propelled forward by environment. A healthy visual and cultural environment breeds confidence in individuality, intellect, and common sense. Sitting at the solar plexus chakra of the business, it's environment that gives people permission, protection, and freedom to move the business forward.

_____ Everyone in the business respects personal boundaries, and understands when boundaries are necessary.

_____ Everyone in the business knows and honors their personal values.

_____ People in the business don't hold grudges, don't gossip, and forgive easily.

_____ Leaders respect people's right to state their opinions and needs as well as challenge feedback that doesn't fit.

_____ Everyone in the business respects each other, and it's apparent by the emotions and actions demonstrated throughout the business.

_____ The environment of the business is open and equal.

_____ The environment of the business promotes creativity and people's needs to be surrounded by light, nature, and color.

_____ When walking through the business, it's visually apparent that everyone is treated equally regardless of position.

_____ The business encourages people to exercise their personal power.

_____ Everyone in the business feels accepted and valued.

Total # of *T*s: _____

Principle #7: Human connectivity is the source of energy.

We are all one and interconnected through energy. We feel what's going on around us, and the result is either inspiration or depletion. Sitting at the sacral chakra of the business, the home of emotion and relationship, business transparency fuels this energy center.

_____ Everyone in the business is respectful during conversations, and only use their phones, laptops, or tablets when absolutely necessary.

_____ Everyone always attends meetings in person when they're in the same building where the meeting is occurring.

_____ During meetings, people are engaged and present, and choose to close their laptops and turn off their phones out of respect.

_____ Leaders in the business clearly understand how to build authentic relationships.

_____ Leaders in the business genuinely care about the people who work in the business.

_____ Everyone in the business is respected for their differences, and discrimination and judgment are never a challenge.

_____ The business clearly has a "Put People First" policy that's apparent in all leadership behaviors throughout the business.

_____ Everyone in the business is encouraged to own their own personal life stories, and the business respects and genuinely appreciates how people's stories shape their skills, knowledge, and abilities.

_____ The business never engages in evil—that includes discrimination, judgments, and doing harm to our Earth or people.

_____ Everyone in the business is encouraged to "disconnect" from work when they leave the office.

Total # of _Ts_: _____

Principle #8: Humanity is the future.

Improving the health and well-being of humanity is the only way to preserve a world that will continue to fuel business. The root chakra of your business is where the basic human needs of people are met, where physical safety and financial security are provided.

_____ The business operates on a "We are one, we are all connected" philosophy.

_____ Leaders clearly understand what it means to have a business that operates with collective responsibility.

_____ Leaders in the business are inspiring. They understand that the business will move forward faster when everyone, regardless of role, is working together as one.

_____ The business clearly takes care of the basic needs of all people. This includes but is not limited to health insurance, fair pay, and equal opportunity.

_____ People in the business are paid fairly and equally for the roles and responsibilities they perform.

_____ The business exercises high moral conduct, never engages in evil activity, and respects both humanity and our Earth.

_____ The business promotes health and wellness by offering organic food options and fresh water for everyone, and encourages people to go on walks and take care of themselves.

_____ The business has a social responsibility program that takes care of humanity and our Earth, a program everyone in the business is proud to be part of.

_____ Everyone in the business works hard but has fun, laughs, and enjoys working together.

Total # of *T*s: _____

Scoring

In the following score sheet document the total number of True statements you identified for each of the Eight Principles of Business. In the column next to the number of True statements identified, multiply the number of True statements by 10 to get a percentage. For example, nine true statements would turn equal 90 percent. Once you have a percentage for each principle, average all of your percentages (add them all up, and then divide by 8) to obtain your energy spectrum percentage.

When developing your business plan for creating your healthy energy ecosystem, you'll want to prioritize your efforts based on where you're seeing the greatest deficiencies. That being said, Principle #1 is your greatest priority and needs to be your first priority, no matter what. Even if the other principles seem easier for your business to attain, if your Principle #1 score is less than 90 percent the other principles will not work, and you will continue having toxic energy pumped into your business. Leadership functionality is number one.

Principle	Business Chakra	Total Number of *T*s	Percentage
Principle #1	Crown Chakra		
Principle #2	Third Eye Chakra		
Principle #3	Throat Chakra		
Principle #4	Thymus Chakra		
Principle #5	Heart Chakra		
Principle #6	Solar Plexus Chakra		
Principle #7	Sacral Chakra		
Principle #8	Root Chakra		
Average Percentage			

Results

90–100 percent

If your business scored 90 to 100 percent you are well on your way. Great job! Your work is simply to maintain the great things you're already doing. Additionally, you have now reached a place of mentorship. It's a responsibility for all businesses who have attained a position of healthy energy to mentor those businesses that are still struggling with dysfunctional practices. You have also now moved into a place of advocacy, and your workplace example can be used to help influence dysfunctional businesses to change; to make a choice to create a business that is fueled with healthy energy. Thank you for your efforts and your future contribution to the world.

80–90 percent

If your business scored 80–90 percent you're almost there. Keep up the great work. This score indicates that you still have work to do, and there may be pockets of your business that are more troublesome than others. This is normal. In many businesses, when an energy ecosystem is being built, some functions within the business will become early adopters and will blaze forward on the trail of healthy energy. Other functions in your business may be struggling in implementing the practices and processes, haven't fully embraced the energy principles, or are dysfunctional and need added support to turn the corner. You may want to consider partnering business functions that are categorized as early adopters with other, less accepting functions. Healthy energy is infectious, and the extra boost of energy may be just what the other functions within your business need to get moving. Don't get frustrated; you're extremely close to the finish line!

70–80 percent

If your business scored 70 to 80 percent your business is teetering and has quite a few pockets of toxic energy flowing through its hallways. This is the most typical starting place for businesses when they begin building their energy ecosystem. If you're like most businesses in this category, leadership dysfunction is your number-one culprit. In fact, you may be doing a lot of things right. The practices in this book may represent some of the practices happening in your business right now, but leadership dysfunction is overshadowing the great amount of effort others are putting into the business. In this category, you may also have mixed emotions circulating through the business. Some people may feel great; others are constant doom and gloom. Together with leadership functionality, personal power and boundaries are a necessary starting point for many businesses within the 70–80 percent range.

>70 percent

If your business scored less than 70 percent, your business is toxic, and it's harmful to the people working within it. Here's the deal: A great number of businesses fall within this category. Your business can no doubt change, pull through, and turn its toxic energy into healthy, life-giving energy that energizes people, ignites action, and drives profits. You just have some work ahead of you. If this is your business, you need to follow every process and practice within this book to a T, and your number-one priority and challenge will be leadership functionality. Energy work is a non-negotiable in order to turn the corner, and it's highly recommended that you hire outside support to move you through the process. Also look to those business chakras where you are doing well, because the strengths within those chakras will give you insight into how the business can leverage the things it's already doing well in order to successfully pull itself forward. Good energy is on its way, you just need to exercise patience, perseverance, and persistence. Good luck!

index

about the author

Gina Soleil is the CEO of Monarch Leadership, a culture development company, and Booya! Worldwide, a humanitarian organization dedicated to improving the health and well-being of humanity. For nearly two decades, Gina has been leading teams through transformational change, and developing high-performing leaders within companies such as Best Buy, UnitedHealth Group, and Caribou Coffee Company.

Gina now advises leaders on how to accelerate business performance by refueling the greatest resource of our time: human energy. Gina has a master's degree in organizational leadership/strategic management and a bachelor's degree in professional communications/training and adult development. She lives in Minneapolis, Minnesota.

Her Website is *www.ginasoleil.com*.